CAMBRIDGE LIBRARY COLLECTION

Books of enduring scholarly value

History

The books reissued in this series include accounts of historical events and movements by eye-witnesses and contemporaries, as well as landmark studies that assembled significant source materials or developed new historiographical methods. The series includes work in social, political and military history on a wide range of periods and regions, giving modern scholars ready access to influential publications of the past.

Magdalen College, Oxford

First published in 1907 as part of the celebrated 'College Monographs' series, *Magdalen College, Oxford* leads readers through the tumultuous and distinguished history of one of Oxford University's most famous institutions. Elected President of Magdalen at the early age of 32, for the rest of his life Thomas Herbert Warren nurtured a passionate enthusiasm for the college, its architecture and traditions. His delight in presiding over such a venerable foundation is evident in his celebratory account of its various 'worthy' alumni including Wolsey, Gibbon and Addison. However, his pride and loyalty did not prevent Warren from committing to paper a number of less prestigious but equally intriguing moments in the college's rich history. From the 'good cheer and bad speeches' experienced in Hall, to the 'delinquencies and debts' of undergraduates, and evidence of dons practising the black arts, Warren's volume still offers readers more than the average college history.

T0382127

Cambridge University Press has long been a pioneer in the reissuing of out-of-print titles from its own backlist, producing digital reprints of books that are still sought after by scholars and students but could not be reprinted economically using traditional technology. The Cambridge Library Collection extends this activity to a wider range of books which are still of importance to researchers and professionals, either for the source material they contain, or as landmarks in the history of their academic discipline.

Drawing from the world-renowned collections in the Cambridge University Library, and guided by the advice of experts in each subject area, Cambridge University Press is using state-of-the-art scanning machines in its own Printing House to capture the content of each book selected for inclusion. The files are processed to give a consistently clear, crisp image, and the books finished to the high quality standard for which the Press is recognised around the world. The latest print-on-demand technology ensures that the books will remain available indefinitely, and that orders for single or multiple copies can quickly be supplied.

The Cambridge Library Collection will bring back to life books of enduring scholarly value (including out-of-copyright works originally issued by other publishers) across a wide range of disciplines in the humanities and social sciences and in science and technology.

Magdalen College, Oxford

T. Herbert Warren

CAMBRIDGE UNIVERSITY PRESS

Cambridge, New York, Melbourne, Madrid, Cape Town, Singapore,
São Paolo, Delhi, Dubai, Tokyo

Published in the United States of America by Cambridge University Press, New York

www.cambridge.org
Information on this title: www.cambridge.org/9781108017954

© in this compilation Cambridge University Press 2010

This edition first published 1907
This digitally printed version 2010

ISBN 978-1-108-01795-4 Paperback

The College

Monographs

THE COLLEGE
MONOGRAPHS
Edited and Illustrated by
EDMUND H. NEW

TRINITY COLLEGE,
CAMBRIDGE
            W. W. ROUSE BALL.
ST. JOHN'S COLLEGE,
CAMBRIDGE
            THE SENIOR BURSAR.
KING'S COLLEGE,
CAMBRIDGE
            C. R. FAY.
MAGDALEN COLLEGE,
OXFORD
            THE PRESIDENT.
NEW COLLEGE,
OXFORD
            A. O. PRICKARD.
MERTON COLLEGE,
OXFORD
            REV. H. J. WHITE.

MAGDALEN COLL: TOWER

MAGDALEN COLLEGE OXFORD

BY

T. HERBERT WARREN

PRESIDENT

(VICE-CHANCELLOR OF THE UNIVERSITY)

ILLUSTRATED BY

EDMUND H. NEW

1907 : LONDON : J. M. DENT & CO.
NEW YORK : E. P. DUTTON & CO.

" *We had neither daylight nor moonlight to see the view of Oxford from the Maudlin Bridge, which I used to think one of the most beautiful in the world.*"

SIR WALTER SCOTT's *Journal*, 1826.

PREFACE

EVERY one who desires to read, much more to write, the history of Magdalen College, will find himself under special obligation to three men, all at different times Fellows of the College—Dr. J. R. Bloxam, Dr. W. D. Macray, and Mr. H. A. Wilson. The more he himself comes to know, the more fully will he appreciate the merit of their work, and the deeper will be his sense of gratitude. These pages are indeed little more than an attempt to popularise some of the results of their solid and conscientious labours. To the pious memory of the first, Dr. Bloxam, I would fain add a word of special tribute. He was in this field a genuine pioneer, to whom the College can never be too grateful. An Eastern poet sings, "To the lover of the rose, the very dust of its petals is dear." So was it with Dr. Bloxam and the lilies of Magdalen. Every scrap of the College life and history to him was precious. *Nihil Magdalenense a se alienum putavit.*

To one other source I most willingly acknowledge my indebtedness, namely, to the *Dictionary of National Biography.* How largely that monumental work has extended the possibility, not to say the ease, of any attempt, small or great, to picture the past of England, or make its lost figures live again, only those know who have essayed the task.

T. H. W.

THE LODGINGS, MAGDALEN COLLEGE,
January 1907.

CONTENTS

CHAPTER I

FOUNDATION AND FIRST YEARS OF THE COLLEGE

CHAPTER II

TUDOR AND STUART TIMES

CONTENTS

CHAPTER III

FROM CROMWELL TO VICTORIA

CONTENTS

CHAPTER IV

College Life down the Centuries

CHAPTER V

Magdalen College Customs

CONTENTS

CHAPTER VI

MAGDALEN WORTHIES

CONTENTS

LIST OF ILLUSTRATIONS

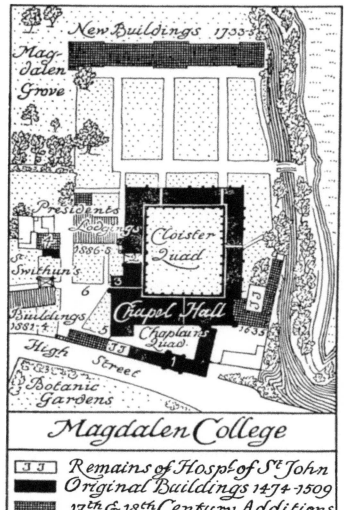

New Buildings 1733-5

Magdalen Grove

Presidents Lodgings 1886-8

Cloister Quad

St. Swithun's

Buildings 1881-4

Chapel Hall 1635

Chaplains Quad.

High Street

Botanic Gardens

Magdalen College

⊓⊓	Remains of Hospl. of St John
▆	Original Buildings 1474-1509
▨	17th & 18th Century Additions
▦	Modern Buildings

1. Great Tower	4 Grammar Hall
2 Founder's „	5 Out-door Pulpit
3 Muniment „	6 St John's Quad.

Magdalen College

CHAPTER I

FOUNDATION AND FIRST YEARS OF THE COLLEGE UNDER THE HOUSES OF LANCASTER AND YORK

THE subtle but compelling beauty and charm of Magdalen College have been so widely recognised, sung, painted, described so often, that it would be a false reticence to ignore them.

The general situation and disposition of the buildings, fortunate and striking, the graceful tower seeming to guard the long, stately bridge and eastern approach to the city, in old days the first object to salute the traveller arriving from London ; the long, low line of walls, roofs, and gables stretching up the street and losing themselves behind aged trees; within, the cloisters with their happy proportion, their sequestered, reposeful air, as of a "garden enclosed," peaceful yet not severe, monastic and domestic at once, the quaint figures on their pedestals standing sentinel round them ;

A

the Chapel with its "storied windows" and "dim religious light," its

> " High embowéd roof,
> And antique pillars massy proof,"

where day after day the listener still hears, as Milton may have done coming in from Horton or Forest Hill,

> " The pealing organ blow
> To the full-voiced choir below " ;

the Founder's Tower with its niched figures and its sumptuous yet delicate and restrained ornament ; the Hall with its carven screen, its moulded and inlaid wainscot, and historic portraits ; the "New Buildings," that "stately pile" to which, recently erected, the priggish genius of Gibbon brought his "stock of erudition that might have puzzled a doctor, and of ignorance of which a schoolboy would have been ashamed " ; the "learned Grove" where the dappled deer flicker in and out amid the towering elms that make its vistas of sombre umbrage and sunny sward ; the little river a natural and delightful moat to the College, to which here it seems wholly to belong ; the bosky "Water-walks" where the memory of Addison yet haunts the favourite spot in which he strolled and discoursed poetry with Harry Sacheverell : all form a harmonious whole, yet a very little consideration shows it to be composed of very different and disparate parts.

2

FOUNDATION

How did it all come together? What have been the annals and fortunes of Magdalen during the four and a half centuries of its existence?

"So venerable, so lovely, steeped in sentiment, . . . spreading her gardens to the moonlight, whispering from her towers the last enchantments of the Middle Age," to no Oxford college do these classic words of Oxford's own poet seem to apply more exactly than to Magdalen.

Yet Magdalen is, in fact, the last of the truly Middle Age colleges, and only just mediæval. If it is not one of the youngest of Oxford foundations, neither is it, as is sometimes supposed, one of the oldest. In point of date it holds an almost absolutely central place among the colleges of Oxford. At the same time, the idea that Magdalen must be older than this, is a natural and not groundless one. For it was established on a site already occupied, and in its establishment absorbed into itself not only the property, but some of the material remains, of a much earlier foundation.

If the visitor who enters the College precincts will stand in the centre of the first quadrangle in which he finds himself, and facing back toward the entrance, turn slowly round, he may read, if he will, the whole history of the College in epitome.

A tombstone in the grass speaks of past generations that have lived and died within the walls. But, in truth, under his feet lie the bones not only of former members of the College but of yet earlier inhabitants of the spot. The quadrangle itself is called St. John's Quadrangle. Imbedded in the low antique line of buildings which separates it from the busy street, are portions of a still more venerable edifice. The beautiful little open-air pulpit, so deftly inserted in the south-east corner, which wakes into life once a year when, on the Festival of St. John Baptist—Midsummer Day—a sermon is preached from it not to the College only, but to the University, joins with its supporting arch the grand College Chapel to a much humbler structure, from which it takes its origin and the quadrangle its name, the Chapel of the Hospital of St. John Baptist.

On the west stands St. Swithun's Quadrangle, the newest of Magdalen "quads," but reviving in its name one of the original College ascriptions. But this again occupies old territory, and embraces part of the site of Magdalen Hall. The modern *grille* links it to a relic of two earlier buildings connected with this foundation, the picturesque "Grammar Hall," with its daintily crocketed, battlemented, and louvred belfry. Opposite to these is the range of the College proper, the west end of the Chapel with its great window only too obviously altered from its original form, and its lovely gateway whose sculptured figures symbolise the history of the College;

4

then the Muniment Tower; the Practice
Room of the Choir, and above it the pro-
jecting windows of the State Bedrooms;
the Founder's Tower; and last, bounding
the northern side, the newest erection in

WEST DOORWAY OF THE CHAPEL

the College, the President's Lodgings, rebuilt in 1886–87.

The entrance gate of the College, it
will be noticed, is of the same date as
St. Swithun's Buildings. Many still living
remember a previous gateway standing
near, but not at the same angle, the much
admired, much criticised Pugin's Gate,

erected in 1844; and there are some yet living who can recall the still earlier and handsome classic portico with its spoked arch, in the style and probably by the hand, of Inigo Jones, which Pugin removed to make way for his own structure.

"In the Name of the holy and undivided Trinity, The Father, The Son, and The Holy Spirit, also of the most blessed Mary Virgin, the glorious blessed Mary Magdalen, Saint John Baptist, the blessed Apostles Peter and Paul, also the glorious Saint Swythun, and other Saints Patrons of our Cathedral Church of Winchester, and of all the Saints of God, we, William Wainfleet, by divine permission Bishop of Winchester, confiding in the goodness of the Supreme Creator of the world, who knows, directs, and disposes the wills of all who trust in Him, out of the good things which in the grace of His fulness He has abundantly bestowed on us in this life, do ordain, institute, found, and establish, by apostolic and royal authority, a perpetual College of poor and needy Scholars, clerks, to study and advance in the School of the University of Oxford in divers sciences and faculties, commonly called *Seynt Marie Maudelyn College in the Université of Oxonford*, to the praise, glory, and honour of the name of the Crucified, and of His most glorious Mother, of the blessed Mary Magdalen, and of all the above Saints, to the maintenance and exaltation of the Christian

6

faith, the setting forward of Holy Church, the increase of divine worship and of the liberal arts, sciences, and faculties."

It is in these words, still preserved in the original Latin form, as the preamble to their nineteenth-century reconstruction, that William Wainfleet commenced his statutes.

But many preliminary steps had been taken before this exalted and happy language could be employed.

At the period when the College was founded, Oxford, like most mediæval cities, was surrounded for purposes of protection by a continuous fortified wall. Of this wall, with its towers and battlements, not a few fragments even now remain. The best are to be found at New College and at Merton College, to which, for this and for many other reasons, the visitor who wishes to understand the "origins" of Magdalen should resort. At New College a considerable and beautiful piece of the wall runs under the Chapel and Hall and surrounds a large part of the garden, following the line of the street still called "Long Wall." At Merton another large fragment, with its bastion and terrace running along "Deadman's Walk," forms in the same way the boundary of the Fellows' Garden, at the corner of which it turns sharply northward at the back of King Street. So it originally continued until, abutting on the High Street, it met the northern line described above, coming down from New College.

MAGDALEN COLLEGE

Here, at what was the eastern boundary of the city, and the main approach from London, it was pierced by a great gate, the site of which is still marked by the "East Gate" Hotel, a modern hostelry signed with an artistic plaque which gives an excellent representation of the East Gate itself.

Outside the gate, where the beautiful Botanic Garden now displays its trim plots, verges, and walks, lay in the earlier part of the fifteenth century what had once been the Jews' Burial Ground. On the other side of the London road stood a low building, its most conspicuous object being the "almshouse," as it was called later, consisting of an unpretending chapel with pointed windows, supported upon a low vaulted stone chamber. To this an arched portal, still to be seen, though built up, in the wall of the College, and known as the "Pilgrim's Gate," gave entrance. Behind might be descried a refectory, a dormitory, stables, a kitchen, and then gardens, or meadows, or waste land, stretching away perhaps as far as where the main stream of the Cherwell divides at what is still called the "King's Mill" in "Mesopotamia."

This was the Hospital of St. John Baptist. It was probably pretty widely known, both from its position at the entrance to Oxford and from its functions. These were, to relieve the sick and to feed the hungry; the hospital of those days combining the

8

offices of the infirmary and the workhouse. Poor scholars and other " miserable persons " of both sexes—for the Hospital contained not only brethren but sisters—were relieved in the " Infirmary." At the " Pilgrim's Gate " already mentioned a dole was dispensed to needy wayfarers.

The Hospital was of considerable antiquity, certainly more than two hundred years old. It was indeed commonly reputed to have been founded by King Henry III. He it was who gave it much of the ground on which it stood, and the mill which still bears his name, and he is said to have laid its foundation-stone with his own hand.

King Richard II. visited it in 1396, on his way from Woodstock to Windsor, and gave in memory of his visit two sets of vestments and a cope.

It was from this Hospital that Wainfleet in 1447 acquired the site of his first foundation, the earlier Magdalen Hall ; not, it should be noted, the site of the present College, then occupied by the Hospital itself, but a parcel of ground within the city wall, lying between the present Examination Schools and Logic Lane.

Of the personal history of the Founder of Magdalen not much is ascertainable. His name was William Patten. He came from the little port of Wainfleet, now known to few, at that time both absolutely and relatively of considerable importance, situate on the Lincolnshire coast of the Wash,

where the little river from the wolds—in its
earlier course the " brook " which flows past
Tennyson's birthplace, and which he loved
so well—enters the sea. His father, Richard
Patten, whose " fair tomb," brought to Oxford in 1830, now reposes in a side shrine
of his son's Chapel, was a gentleman ; his
mother, Margery, daughter of Sir William
Brereton, a lady. His brother John, who
appears in miniature on the same tomb, was
afterwards Archdeacon of Surrey and Dean
of Chichester.

Where William Wainfleet himself was
educated is unknown. He was certainly in
one sense both a Wykehamist and an Etonian,
for he was Headmaster of Winchester School
for twelve years (1429–1441), and in 1441
King Henry VI. transferred him, with a
certain number of his boys, to start, as Headmaster, the sister College of St. Mary the
Virgin of Eton—

> " Mary, in whose fair name was laid
> Eton's corner."

At the end of the next year he was made
Provost. Wainfleet was thus a living link
in the *amicabilis concordia* which has always
united these two foundations. He may
also be said to be a link between New
College and Magdalen. For if William
of Wainfleet did not immediately succeed
William of Wykeham, he certainly followed
closely and lovingly upon his footsteps.
Forty-two years had elapsed from the passing

away of that great pioneer Founder, though only one Prelate had since sat on his throne, when, upon the death of Cardinal Beaufort in 1447, Wainfleet was at once chosen and elected, at the recommendation of King Henry himself, Bishop of Winchester, and was consecrated in the new and beautiful Chapel of Eton College.

Less than a year later he obtained a patent authorising him to found a Hall, consisting of a President and fifty scholars, for the study of Theology and Philosophy in the University of Oxford. The conception was probably no new one with him. When King Henry VI. mooted the project of founding a College, Wainfleet, it is said, tried to persuade him to found it at Oxford. Had he succeeded, Cambridge would have lost "King's," and Oxford might have lost Magdalen. But King Henry replied, "Nay, rather at Cambridge, that I may have two universities in my realm."

What he had not been able to persuade the King to effect, Wainfleet (as perhaps the King foresaw would follow), being now in a position to do so, proceeded at once to carry out himself.

The relation of Magdalen Hall to St. John's Hospital has been already indicated. Eight years later he became Lord Chancellor, and with the same promptitude at once began to put a further plan into execution. Within a few days he sought and obtained the patronage of the Hospital, and next year, 1457, received the licence to found, and founded, on the site of the Hospital, the College of St. Mary Magdalen.

But Magdalen, like Rome, was not to be built in a day. Another ten years were to elapse before Wainfleet could even begin to place one stone upon another. It was a troubled and uncertain time, that of the Wars of the Roses. Two years after his foundation was complete on parchment, the House of Lancaster, to which Wainfleet was attached, fell on the stricken field of Northampton, and the Bishop had to make his submission to Edward IV. Some advantage the years of waiting and the ill wind of war blew to his College.

A certain Sir John Fastolf, a rich and robustious Norfolk knight who had fought in the French wars, had built himself a huge castle at Caister, and was, as it was becoming the fashion to be, something of a patron of letters, left provision in his will for the foundation of a college at Caister, for seven priests and seven poor folk. The will was disputed and said to be a forgery of John Paston, one of the well-known letter-writing east-country family. The story of the dispute is long and complicated. In the result, Sir John's foundation was annexed to Magdalen College. His seven priests were represented by the four Chaplains and three of the Fellows, his seven poor folk by seven of the Demies. Whether Sir John Fastolf gave his name to Sir John Falstaff

has been and will be disputed ; but the latter
knight certainly gave a sobriquet to the
foundationers of the former when, more than
a century later, the College jest arose which
dubbed Fastolf's seven Demies "Buckram
men."

Wainfleet managed then to approve himself to the reigning powers, though not
without due propitiation. In 1467 he
obtained a confirmation of his charters, and
he now began to break ground.

Wainfleet's first care was his boundary
wall. The College, it will be remembered,
stood outside the *enceinte* of the city, and
required fortifications of its own. The
fine crenellated wall, with its angle tower,
is no mere ornament. It was intended to
serve, and has served, as a genuine defensive
work.

> "And lest unruly ruffians might offend
> Their studious minds, he hath encompassed round
> The College with a wall which might defend
> His scholars both from fear of any wound,
> And make resistance 'gainst an army's might,
> And, ere our valour-murdering guns were found,
> Did well perform that charge ; for I dare write,
> The students with few friends but meanly strong
> Might have maintained it 'gainst a kingdom's wrong."
> HEYLIN'S *Memorial of Wainfleet.*

Begun in 1467, it took some years to complete. Six years later the building of the
College proper began very appropriately with
the Chapel. The foundation-stone was laid
on May 5, 1473, by the first President,
William Tybard, and blessed by Robert

Toly, Bishop of St. David's; the good Bishop, as the College accounts show, being entertained at breakfast on the occasion.

In 1479 the Chapel, Hall, and Cloisters were approaching completion, and they were probably practically finished by the summer of the next year, 1480.

This same year saw also the commencement of the Grammar School of the College. The Founder was himself an old schoolmaster with experience of two great schools. He recognised that a large number of the students who came to Oxford required a preliminary grounding before they could with profit attend the University courses which he was providing in his College.

He now erected within the boundary wall of his territory, and over against the College itself, a school with a Grammar Master and Usher. All was on a very handsome scale. The schoolroom was some seventy feet in length, about the same as that at Eton. The payments of the Master and Usher were liberal, and the two men whom Wainfleet secured as his first appointments, John Anwykyll and John Stanbridge, left their mark on the national education. Indeed, through Lilly, they may be said to have started the general tradition of the Grammar Schools and the Latin Grammars of England. For Lilly's Grammar travelled not only to St. Paul's and Eton, but to schools like that of Stratford-on-Avon. From it Shakespeare learnt his "*Hic, hæc, hoc,*" being taught it in all probability by an old pupil of Wainfleet's school at Magdalen, one Roche of Corpus Christi College.

With such teachers, the school at once attracted pupils from the academic body throughout Oxford, and, in some way not recorded, a Hall grew up at its doors, on a site leased by the College, the later "Magdalen Hall." It held its ground under the shadow of the College for some three hundred and twenty years, and then removing to the site and buildings of Hart Hall, still kept its name, until within recent memory both were merged in the refounded Hertford College.

Of the buildings both of the Grammar School and Magdalen Hall portions have been at different times pulled down, but the greater part was destroyed by a fire in the first quarter of the last century. The much-admired little building known as the "Grammar Hall" preserves the only fragments which remain, and the name and tradition of both.

Magdalen College was now complete. It remained to give it its constitution, and the body of statutes under which it was to live. The Founder has been called a Wykehamist, and, like the Wykehamist Chicheley at All Souls, in his buildings he followed the general lines of New College, though these were modified, partly by the desire for improvement, partly probably in view of the existing buildings of St. John's

Hospital. In his statutes he again followed Wykeham, though with differences. Magdalen, like New College, was to consist of a Head and seventy scholars, a scriptural and

THE GRAMMAR HALL

sacred number ; but, unlike Wykeham's scholars, those of Wainfleet were divided into two bodies, the full Fellows and the half Fellows or Demies, and these latter

16

were distinctly recognised as junior scholars pursuing junior studies.

The essential characteristic of Wainfleet's foundation is its careful elaboration and gradation, with the provision of suitable teaching at each grade, and the fact that both the highest and the lowest teaching were thrown open without payment to all members of the University. The Grammar Master and Usher provided a due grounding in Grammar. The instruction in the next stage, that of Logic and Sophistry, was furnished by the College lecturers. Finally, for the highest study there were the three Præ-lectors in the three subjects of Theology and of Natural and Moral Philosophy. These were practically University teachers, though appointed by the College. Their lectures were open to members of other colleges, and they were, in fact, an anticipa-tion of the Professorial and Intercollegiate as distinguished from the College system. In this at any rate Wainfleet can lay claim to originality, and may be pronounced a real pioneer in the higher education of his country. The importance which he him-self attached to his " Readers " is shown by the high rate of pay which he assigned to them. The Choir at Magdalen, as at New College, was from the first intended to be of great importance.

The bulk of the statutes were ready when the College was finished to receive them in the summer of 1480. But the first President,

17   B

William Tybard, was hardly the man to carry them out. He was not used to statutes; he had governed the College for some twenty years without any, and he was old and breaking in health. The Founder thought it well to find a fresh man to inaugurate the new rule. His choice fell on Dr. Richard Mayew, a former Fellow of New College, who appeared with the Founder's mandate, and was admitted President at the end of August 1480.

A year later the Founder himself came and paid a long visit. He brought with him title-deeds for the Muniment Room and 800 volumes for the Library. He was received in state with a procession and a congratulatory speech by the President. Two days later he set out towards Woodstock to meet King Edward IV., who volunteered a promise that he would come and visit the newly-built College and spend the night there. "*Quæ res,*" as the College chronicler remarks, "*non mediocriter complacuit domino Fundatori.*"

"Accordingly," as he goes on, "that same night after sunset our most illustrious Lord the King was first of all received in state with a multitude of lights outside the University by the Lord Chancellor of the University and the regent and non-regent Masters of Arts, and next was received in state with a procession into the College of the Blessed Mary Magdalen by the Lord Founder and the President and Scholars,

and spent the night there with a number
of Lords temporal and Spiritual, and stayed
till after lunch next day."

The chronicler proceeds to narrate how,
this next day being Sunday, between Matins
and Procession the President once more
made a brief little congratulatory speech to
the King, asking his special favour to the
University and the College. The King
replied "amply and aptly" to everything,
and granted the petitions. He then in state,
with his lords, followed the procession round
the College cloisters.

Less than two years later the College saw
a still more exciting royal visit. This time
the Founder came up on St. Mary Magdalen's Day to receive the King on his
way to Woodstock. Once more the King
was first of all received outside the University by the Chancellor and Masters, then
brought in processional state into the College, with his attendant Bishops and Lords
Temporal, who all slept in College. But
though some of the Lords and Bishops were
the same, the monarch was a new one,
Richard III., the brother of the King who
had been fêted so recently, the guardian,
and in popular repute the murderer, of his
son. Dr. Goldwin Smith argues that this
special reception by the Founder is evidence
that Richard was not quite the monster that
he has sometimes been represented. Be
that as it may, the conjunction is certainly
a striking one, and the picture of President

and Fellows, headed by their venerable and benevolent Founder, now over eighty years of age, meeting the sinister figure of Richard Crookback at the gates of Oxford and filing into their College, its beautiful buildings still crisp and white in the July sun, is one that appeals to the imagination. Whether it was worth his while to receive the approval of the Founder or no, the famous or infamous monarch was pleased to be gracious and displayed much royal tact. He stayed two nights, and on the second day called for solemn disputations in Hall and rewarded the disputants—among whom it may be noted was William Grocyn, now Reader in Theology—with gifts of venison and money. He also gave the President and Fellows two bucks and five marks for wine. " May the King live for ever ! " the College chronicler concludes. He seems to have come again in the autumn, and made an offering at the College altar of 6s. 8d., apparently the usual royal oblation. Two years later Wainfleet is found lending the King £100 ; but a Lancastrian at heart, he probably did not regret overmuch the loss of his loan when Bosworth Field avenged Northampton, and he was careful to order President Mayew to attend the coronation of Henry of Richmond.

On August 11, 1486, the Founder passed away. He had not ceased to interest himself in his College or to add to its endowment. In particular he had attached to it the revenues of several small foundations in different parts of the country, the Hospital of Romney, the Chapel of St. Katherine at Wanborough, the Hospitals of St. John and St. James at Brackley and Aynho, and the Priory of Selborne. By his will he left still further benefactions, making it indeed his chief legatee. Three carts brought his furniture and various personal belongings from Waltham to the College, at a cost of £6, 3s. 4d., including his staff, mitre, and other ornaments. Less happy or less cautious than New College, Magdalen has lost mitre and staff, and the only relics of this kind that now remain to her are his sandals and buskins and some pieces of an embroidered vestment. He sleeps in his beautiful chantry Chapel of St. Mary Magdalen in his own Cathedral Church of Winchester, but his fairest and most living and lasting monument is the College which he endowed with such princely prudence and generosity.

CHAPTER II

MAGDALEN COLLEGE UNDER THE TUDORS
AND STUARTS ; THE REFORMATION AND
THE CIVIL WAR

A COLLEGE may be said to come of age
when its founder dies. Magdalen
was now fairly launched. Its President,
Mayew, was a man of mark. He stood
well with the new monarch, Henry VII. ;
and if that parsimonious Welshman, the
first English King who understood the
value of money, made but "a frugal offering" at the College altar, it is perhaps
all the more significant that he appointed
President Mayew his Almoner and employed
him on business of different kinds. He not
only invited the President to Windsor, but
visited the College himself, and also let his
eldest son, a delicate boy, who was very
precious to him and to his mother, Arthur,
Prince of Wales, pay two visits and reside
with Dr. Mayew in his Lodgings. The
President again was employed in negotiat-
ing the ill-starred alliance with Princess
Katharine of Arragon ; two Spanish Am-
bassadors and the Spanish Nuncio are found
dining about this time in the College, and
later, when the wedding took place, some

Cloisters & founder's Tower

tapestry representing the occasion was presented to the Lodgings, where it still hangs.

It consists of four chief pieces ; in one of these the parties to the wedding seem to be grouped to right and left of a central royal figure—King Henry VII. ?—in another are seen a number of ladies and an ecclesiastic with a book, waiting behind a barrier, while at the side is a fountain flowing with wine. The third shows several couples seated in state, (?) the King and Queen, Prince and Princess, and their suite. The fourth, a singularly charming and artistic piece, sometimes called the " Labourers in the Vineyard," represents the process of making wine, gathering grapes, squeezing them in a press and drawing off the liquor. In front is a young princely figure, paying, or giving largess to, a kneeling labourer.

The buildings of the College, too, were now finished off, by the completion of the southern walk of the Cloister under the Chapel and Hall. Above all, that beautiful and notable feature of the College and of Oxford, without which it is difficult to imagine either, the Great or Bell Tower, was now erected. It was begun in 1492, but was not ready to receive the bells till well into the next century, 1505. About this date a mason, a painter, and a beer-brewer contracted to make a clock for the College, warranting it to go truly for "a year and a day."

The College, moreover, was full of life

and vigour, many students of subsequent
distinction entering it, among them not a
few who became prominent in the stirring
times so soon to follow, notably Thomas
Wolsey, and possibly also John Colet.

But perhaps President Mayew was too
much occupied with public and other affairs
outside the College ; anyhow, signs of
disorder and discontent began to manifest
themselves. They culminated when the
President, after being appointed Bishop of
Hereford, still continued to hold the presidency ; and a year or two later the authority
of the Visitor was invoked, and Dr. Mayew,
who had reigned more than a quarter of a
century, was compelled to resign.

Mayew's successor was Dr. John Claymond, certainly one of the most memorable
of all Oxford Heads of Houses. He had
held several pieces of preferment ; he was
the friend of Erasmus and More, and known
to scholars all over Europe ; he was very
wealthy ; what is more, he was a most pious
and charitable man, "full of good works
and alms-deeds which he did." But he
was not long to remain at Magdalen. He
had been a protégé of Bishop Fox, who was
now himself following in the footsteps of
Wykeham and Wainfleet and founding a
College, the first College, as it has been
called, of the Renaissance, the College of
Corpus Christi. It is a double tribute to
Magdalen that Fox should have chosen its
President to rule over his new Society, and

should have thought at once that this was the best thing he could do for Corpus and that Magdalen could bear the loss. But, stranger still, the compliment was to be repeated, and almost immediately. Claymond was succeeded at Magdalen by John Higdon, but Higdon in his turn was requisitioned by a greater man and for a greater charge. When Wolsey, now the foremost figure in Church and State, established his magnificent "Cardinal College," afterward refounded as Christ Church, he appointed John Higdon to be its first Dean, with four Fellows of Magdalen as four of his Canons.

The daughter, in a sense, of New College, Magdalen had thus, less than fifty years from her birth, become in her turn the mother of two new foundations. She had, too, already given to the world not a few who had done eminent service in Church and State. She had good reason to be pleased with herself. Disorders and discontents, it is true, had manifested themselves. Her strict rule, her semi-monastic life, were perhaps hardly suited to the times, already full of ferment. But at this moment the College had the sense of being in the van of a movement full of hope and promise—the movement of the English as distinguished from the Italian Renaissance, of the English as distinguished from the German Reformation. We may well imagine that in these early years of Henry VIII., that paragon and pillar as he was deemed of Christendom, with the sunshine of the great Cardinal's favour upon his College, and the intoxication of the New Learning working in his brain, carried away in fancy and feeling by the sudden rise of England and the rapid growth of Oxford, many a young scholar of Magdalen felt himself "standing on the top of golden hours."

> " Bliss was it in that hour to be alive,
> But to be young was very heaven."

They were in truth, like the generation for which these lines were written, on the eve of a Revolution, though carried on under the forms of law.

The next fifty years were to prove a most troubled and appalling time of discord and of destruction, in which Magdalen's sons were to see their fair College suffer in proportion to its beauty and completeness. Wolsey's tragic fall was to follow in two years' time, his sad death a year later. In point of fact, the changes which brought on the Reformation had begun, and in all Wolsey's colleges, in Magdalen, in Corpus, and in Christ Church.

It is a symptom that in 1521 Wolsey had called for four divines to be sent by the University to London to consult as to the best means of checking the spread of Lutheran doctrines in England, and that three out of the four sent were Magdalen men. But it was Wolsey's own foundation, with the number of Cambridge men it

28

introduced, which had brought Lutheranism into Oxford.

Magdalen Hall, where William Tyndale held his Bible readings, was the focus, but Tyndale and his views had friends in the College as well as in the Hall. For a time the spread of the movement seems to have been checked. The English Reformation proceeded, as is well known, on other lines and by other agencies. The question of the King's divorce, the question of the King's supremacy as Head of the English Church, both touched the College, the latter intimately.

The dissolution and suppression of the religious houses affected all the colleges, with which they were allied both directly and indirectly, and can hardly have failed to cause them much concern. A record of the period in Magdalen is possibly to be found in the panelling over the daïs in the College Hall. The wainscoting generally appears to have been introduced in 1541. The little carved insets in the centre over the High Table represent the acts of St. Mary Magdalen. In the middle of these, in the place of honour, is the florid, rubicund effigy of King Henry VIII. It is said that the panelling, or part of it, originally belonged to Reading Abbey, which had just been dissolved. If this is so, the irony of history is strikingly exemplified. But this is not certain. The carvings were certainly put up in the days of Thomas Cromwell, but the accounts show the panelling to have been bought in London.

In the same year in which this wainscoting was introduced, large sums were spent on vestments for the Chapel. The College then was materially prosperous, and able to pursue the tenor of its own life. The old order on the whole maintained itself, though there were serious differences and violent and unseemly demonstrations of disagreement within its body, invading the Chapel itself. How high matters ran may be seen when it is recorded that one young Fellow, a good Greek scholar and afterwards a bishop, could, in the sight of a large congregation, on "Whitsun Eavin," go to the "high Aulter" and "most unreverently" take away the Sacrament and break it in pieces ; and that another, a Bachelor of Arts, could "pull a Priest from the aulter after he was past the Gospel and fling away his book."

But with Edward VI. a sweeping innovation was brought in which changed the whole face of religious life and worship in the College, and affected its daily tenor in many ways, abolishing, for instance, fasting on Fridays, the practice of the tonsure, and the wearing of the old monastic dress.[1]

The story is a long and sad one. It can be traced imperfectly from the College

---

[1] "Chymericos habitus prodigiosasque vestes posthac gestet nemo." " Togas in antica parte consui vetamus." So runs one of the Edwardian injunctions.

accounts. Suffice it to say that the College
was attacked by a mob ; that the President
was arraigned for ritualism ; that first the

A CORNER OF THE CLOISTERS

side altars were destroyed and then even the
high altar itself ; that images, pictures, ornaments were removed wholesale, together

with the organ ; and that a Cambridge man, the Master of Trinity Hall, was forced upon the College as President, who sold the vestments and furniture of the Chapel.

Then under Queen Mary the ancient order was for a while reinstated. The same carpenter or designer, Henry Bolton, who had supplied the College with a Communion Table, was now employed to restore the images in the Chapel. Owen Oglethorpe, the old President, was brought back, and it was the turn of the Lutheran party to take flight. But Oxford colleges have always been tolerant. Leave of absence was given to them to pursue research abroad, and if the College entertained the Commissioners appointed to dispute with Cranmer, Ridley, and Latimer, it also entertained Dr. Haddon, the former intruded President who had sold the vestments. A piece of tapestry cloth, still used to cover the High Table at College meetings, is said to date from Queen Mary's reign.

When Elizabeth came to the throne, Magdalen no doubt, like Oxford and the rest of the country, held its breath for a while in anxious suspense. Would the old order continue or no ? Would she be Protestant or Roman or Anglican ? What was her religion ? Perhaps, like " that of all sensible men," it was never known. It was certainly not known at her accession. Meantime it was an unsettled and unsettling time, which showed itself in a good deal of petty brawling. Very slowly the ground-swell subsided. A Commission was sent to regulate matters. Once more the altars and images were removed from the Chapel. More gradually, it would seem, the services were altered.

When the Visitor came in September 1561, he found " the Colledge of Mawdlens thoroly conformable," willing generally to accept the Queen's supremacy, the Book of Common Prayer, and the Queen's injunctions. He thought it best to deprive the Marian President Coveney, " lest a great many of the most handsome [1] young men should have departed and left the house as they playnly sayd they wolde in case he contynued head there, so manifestly both unworthie and enfringing the Statutes of the Colledge." A successor was found in the redoubtable Dr. Laurence Humfrey, Regius Professor of Divinity, an able and learned divine who had come back from Zurich, bringing with him a wife, a Geneva gown, and the tenets of Calvin. Of these tenets he had the courage ; he removed the last traces of the "superstitious" altars and ornaments, introduced a pulpit, and fitted up the Chapel to the north of the Choir with benches for Mistress Humfrey, and he pulled down the ancient cross in the High Street opposite the Pilgrims' Gate, dating from the old Hospital of St. John.

[1] *i.e.* well affected ; "handsome is that handsome does."

An interesting and notable figure in the line of Presidents is that of Laurence Humfrey. Strong, vigorous, black-avised, as he looks down from his "comely monument" in the Ante-Chapel or out of his portrait, a learned man, a man of the world, but stiff and self-important, not altogether pleasant, unintentionally not unamusing. He complained that the presidentship was "more worshippful than profitable, more painful than gayneful." He would not at first conform. He was with difficulty persuaded to adopt the surplice or even the academic habit. But Queen Elizabeth took his measure. When he went out to meet her at Woodstock in his scarlet, while he was kissing her hand, she said, "Dr. Humfrey, methinks this gown and habit become you very well, and I marvel that you are so strait-laced on this point—but I come not now to chide." What she would have said had she seen Mistress Humfrey in her pew in the Chapel may perhaps be guessed from her speech to the wife of Archbishop Parker.

Gradually he became more willing to conform. He was talked of for a bishopric, and he was actually made Dean, first of Gloucester and afterward of Winchester.

He filled the College with pupils and protégés of his own. These were Commoners, and were not supposed to be under the jurisdiction of the College officers. They did not cap the Fellows when they met them. Many of them were rich and of good family. The rich apparently drew poor ones after them, or else Humfrey somehow made the rich support the poor. Anyhow, they were a somewhat miscellaneous and disorderly set. The Fellows, like those in Bentley's day at Trinity, Cambridge, found them a nuisance, and complained that they turned the College into a chaos or an anarchy. "All things, places, persons are full of disorder and confusion," they wrote, "and our Colledge like to that Commonwealth wherein it was said, ἀκούει οὐδεὶς οὐδὲν οὐδένος."

They went deer-stealing in Shotover Forest, and one of them was imprisoned for this by Lord Norris, the Lord-Lieutenant of the county. When Lord Norris came to Oxford they organised an attack upon him at the Bear Inn, near All Saints' Church, where he was staying. A free fight ensued, in which, before the Vice-Chancellor and Proctors could stop it, some of the scholars were hurt, and my Lord's keeper, "Binks," was sorely wounded. The Vice-Chancellor ordered the scholars to be gated in College while Lord Norris was to leave the town. But the young men "went up to the top of their tower, and waiting till he should pass by towards Ricot, sent down a shower of stones that they had picked up upon him and his retinue, wounding some and endangering others of their lives. It is said that upon the foresight of this storm divers had got boards, others tables on their

35

heads to keep them from it, and that if the Lord had not been in his coach or chariot he would certainly have been killed."

After this they were naturally "sent down," some of them for good, and Lord Norris was pacified, though "with much ado, by the sages of the University."

It is only fair to say, however, that if the College under President Humfrey was rather "rowdy," there were among these Commoners several who made their mark, notably Sir Thomas Bodley, one of Humfrey's first pupils; John Lyly, the author of *Euphues*; John Florio, a poor scholar in attendance on one Emanuel Barnes, whom he taught Italian; and perhaps William Camden.

When, after twenty-seven years, Humfrey passed away, Queen Elizabeth recommended to the Fellows Dr. Nicholas Bond, one of her Chaplains and a former member of their own body; but the Fellows did not see their way to elect him. The politic Queen, however, did not fall into the mistake afterward made by James II., or else she had more friends in College than he. Her candidate was in every way an eligible and suitable one, and taking advantage of a technical flaw, which perhaps her friends manœuvred to procure, she nominated Bond and he was admitted.

The "Bond of Iniquity" he was called by his Puritan opponents. He seems also, like Sir Christopher Hatton, then Chancellor of the University, the grave Lord Keeper who so happily "led the brawls" while "the seals and maces danced before him," to have been a good "daunser"; and this, too, was cast up against him by the Marprelate writers.

Anyhow, the "Bond of Iniquity" proved an equitable and successful President. The Queen naturally lent him her countenance, and while he was Vice-Chancellor in 1592 visited and was received by him at Oxford. The occasion, of course, produced a Latin poem. But indeed the College was becoming noted as a place of "wits and pens." It flourished; the lecture list was regulated and enlarged; lectures on geography and cosmography were introduced. The Elizabethan spirit seemed to have affected it, and sharing the general prosperity of the times, the College revenues showed a divisible surplus. There was plenty to spend on repairing and embellishing the fabric of the College itself. Notably when King James I. came to visit Oxford in 1605—for the royal favour did not cease with the setting of the "bright occidental star" of Elizabeth—a great deal was done to decorate the Hall and Cloisters. The beautiful Jacobean screen at the entrance of the Hall was probably now erected, and the statues and figures in the Cloisters were certainly painted. Moses, in particular, was given a sky-blue coat. So life-like did he look in this garb, says Wake the chronicler, doubtless repeating a good College story, that a countryman who had blundered into the

Cloisters, and then like many other visitors
lost himself, was actually seen to go up to
him, pull off his cap, and making a profound
obeisance, ask to be shown the way. The
British Solomon, who, if a pedant, was also,
as became the pupil of Buchanan, a scholar
and a poet, rose to the occasion and pronounced Magdalen to be " the most *absolute*
building in Oxford." It should be remembered, however, that one rival at any
rate, a characteristic glory of his own reign,
was not yet built, namely, Wadham College.
More than this, his eldest son, Prince Henry,
a boy of twelve, was entertained in the College of which his Governor, Sir Thomas
Chaloner, was a member. " He sat," says
the chronicler, " all alone in the middle of
the High Table, his suite and the Gentlemen
Commoners in the middle, the students in
academic dress on either side against the
wall. With royal tact he graciously ordered
them to put on their square caps, and then,
seizing a cup foaming with generous wine,
addressed the scholars comprehensively in a
loud voice, and drank to their health, when
immediately all rose to their feet and re-
sponded to the greeting. As he left the
College he said, ' Good-bye, gentlemen !
Good-bye all of you ! ' and he was wont
afterwards to call Magdalen his own College, and to say that he would ever be
mindful of it."

But if the College called him their
" Mæcenas," they had soon, alas ! to call

him their "Marcellus." Like Prince Arthur, the Prince of Wales entertained by the College a hundred years before, he did not survive his first youth. His portrait hangs in the Hall where he displayed his gay boyish camaraderie, and in the Library which he visited with so much interest, reposes, itself now one of the musty, dusty tomes which he said were most to his liking, a volume of verses in Latin, Greek, and Spanish, entitled *Luctus Postumus*, a part of the general mourning of the University and country.

An entry in the College accounts shows that the College spent 30s. on "Blackes" at his funeral. His death, like that of Prince Arthur, was more momentous than they were aware, not so much in the career it cut short as in the career to which it opened up the way. Meanwhile, however, the troubles to which it indirectly led were some way off. The College was, like the bulk of the nation, or at any rate of Parliament, prevailingly Puritan. It was now that George Wither and John Hampden, two of the most shining of her names, entered Magdalen within a few years of each other. When President Bond died, the Fellows elected two Puritan Presidents in succession. When in 1626 they unanimously voted for the Vice-President Accepted Frewen, son of a Puritan rector in Sussex, it might have been thought, to judge by his parentage and his question-begging name, they had elected a third. And indeed, when they had elected him Fellow fourteen years earlier, he was, as Antony Wood says, " Puritanically inclined."

But he had since seen the world ; he had been, like Mayew, concerned in a Spanish marriage, having been Chaplain to the Ambassador, Sir John Digby, one of a family much connected with the College. He was now Reader in Theology, Chaplain to the King and a Canon of Canterbury, and a moderate supporter of Laud.

He took the College Chapel in hand. The floor was repaved, the stalls renewed, the windows of the Ante-Chapel filled with coloured glass—the tracery of the great west window being unfortunately altered to suit the design introduced, perhaps by Christopher Schwarz—the east wall covered with coloured representations of the Nativity, the Passion, the Resurrection, and the Ascension. To Frewen, too, belongs the brass eagle-lectern still to be seen in the Chapel.

The Altar as rearranged by Frewen, the first set up in the University since the Reformation, was compared by some, now more Puritanically inclined than he was, to that at Bethel. The music apparently was much increased.

The great architect of the day, Inigo Jones, was also introduced to the College, to erect a classical entrance gateway, the gable-end of St. John's Hospital and the portico to the Chapel being at the same time brought into harmony with this.

The statues in the Cloisters were again given a coat of paint—Moses doubtless a blue coat—and money was spent in improving the Water Walks. For the better

FIGURE IN THE CLOISTERS

accommodation of the Commoners, a new block of buildings, the Kitchen Staircase, was erected at the east end of the Hall. Their separate Common Room on this staircase continued into the memory of persons yet living, and the set of rooms is still marked by a fine coat of arms which belonged to it in this capacity.

Whatever may have been Laud's demerits, his regulations seem to have stimulated the industry of the Colleges, and of Magdalen among them, so much so that a fashionable young Demy of this time, son of a Secretary of State, is found writing to complain that the new regulations have " taken away all his leisure."

Peaceful, prosperous, studious, its internal brawls and bickerings, as well ecclesiastical as temporal, assuaged, the College seemed pursuing happily the even tenor of its way. But without, a national storm was gathering, soon to break, and when it broke, alike for geographical, social, and ecclesiastical reasons, Magdalen was to be one of the colleges destined to feel it first and most heavily. Many a quiet Demy, meditating his Plato or Aristotle by the banks of Cherwell, or cultivating a peripatetic philosophy in the newly embellished Water Walks, or dreaming, like Wither, of his mistress " Fair Virtue," may have been moved to quote his Horace with new and poignant perception of its force :—

> " Romæ nutriri mihi contigit atque doceri
> Iratus Graiis quantum nocuisset Achilles.
> Adjecere bonæ paulo plus artis Athenæ,
> Scilicet ut possem curvo dignoscere rectum,
> Atque inter silvas Academi quærere verum.
> *Dura sed emovere loco me tempora grato*
> *Civilisque rudem belli tulit æstus in arma.*"
> HORACE, *Epistles*, II. ii. 41–47.

THE CIVIL WAR

Events moved rapidly when they once began to move. In July 1642 the King made his appeal to the College for funds to aid him in the coming struggle. Magdalen promised to raise £1000. Dr. Frewen, the President, advanced £500, and Dr. John Nourse, a Law Fellow, £50. The King issued his proclamations against treason. The London Road by the College was barricaded with long timber logs ; heavy stones—a primitive but, as Lord Norris could testify, not despicable ammunition— were taken up to the top of the Great Tower ; the scholars were enrolled and drilled. On August 28 Sir John Byron arrived in Oxford with a troop of horse to recruit, and after about a fortnight's stay, marched out to join the King. With him went, as volunteers, some hundred scholars, among them the loyal Dr. John Nourse, who was given a command. For him the war was soon over. Six weeks later he fell at Edgehill. That sad fight was only the beginning of woes. Lord Saye and the Parliamentarians, who had meanwhile visited [1] and disarmed Oxford and her colleges, had decided not to hold the city, and King Charles presently made it his headquarters.

Magdalen was now placed regularly in a state of siege. The College plate was

[1] The Parliamentary troops seem to have assaulted the College at their entry, and damaged the Chapel windows very seriously.

sold and melted up.[1] "Ordnance and great guns" had been driven into the Grove at the King's first arrival ; some of these latter were placed on the barricade, which had been strengthened with earth. As matters proceeded stronger measures were taken. The beautiful walks, lately embellished, were with their meadows brought into a state of defence, their trees being sacrificed for this purpose. The little mound still to be seen where the main stream of the Cherwell turns at right angles to flow past the "Angel Meadow," and in which the northern walk, now known as Addison's, ends, took the name apparently of Dover Pier from the Earl of Dover, who commanded the University regiment, and the mound doubtless marks a small battery or bastion.

For the Thames valley between Oxford and London was now the chief theatre of the war. "Sometimes," says a brilliant young writer, Mr. Trevelyan, "Hampden and his troops pounced down from his wooded Chilterns on to the plain below ; or Essex wound in slow pomp of horse, foot, and artillery over the uplands south of Thames. More often Rupert, issuing from the fortress of Magdalen College at the bridge-head, where he was quartered with the hardest riders of the army, could be

[1] The Founder's Cup perhaps survived. Among the pieces disposed of was a *cantharus*, or tankard, presented by John Hampden of Buckinghamshire.

THE CIVIL WAR

seen by the first light of morning, high on Shotover Hill, galloping towards glory and plunder afar."

> "Time passed—my groves were full of warlike stirs.
> The student's heart was with the merry spears,
> Or keeping measure to the clanking spurs
> Of Rupert's cavaliers."
>> ARCHBISHOP ALEXANDER,
>> *Oxford and her Chancellor.*

That Prince Rupert[1] actually resided in the College at this period is not certain, though he was often within its walls, and his trumpeters may, as Macaulay writes, have been "heard calling to horse through its quiet cloisters." Trumpeters now very often appear in the College accounts.

> "Sæpe etiam victis redit in præcordia sanguis,
> Victoresque cadunt Danai;"——

Hampden, who, as his own College was to do a few years later, had appealed from and to a Stuart king in his Courts of Law, and then going further from the gown to the sword, was to wear gown, or see his old College, no more. The obelisk on the "field of Chalgrove" marks where he fell in the early summer of 1643.

> "There on thy musings broke the painful sound
> Of arms; the long-plumed cavaliers
> Clanged through the courts—the low fat fields around
> Were filled with strife and tears."
>> SIR LEWIS MORRIS,
>> *To an Unknown Poet.*

[1] His portrait, a fine one by the contemporary painter Michael Wright, appropriately hangs in the Hall opposite that of his uncle, Henry, Prince of Wales.

45

Amid these distractions the College life was still carried on. The officers held their meetings ; the Dean's writ still ran. A Puritan Demy, Richard Lytcott, had been absent without leave. It appeared that he had been serving as an "Antient" in Lord Peterborough's regiment, against the King. With the sanction of the Visitor, he was deprived as guilty of a "*crimen enorme.*" But it was carried on under difficulties and distractions. Dr. Frewen was consecrated Bishop of Lichfield in the College Chapel on April 28, 1644. His successor, Dr. Oliver, was admitted a month later, on May 28. The first day of his presidency bade fair to find him not merely Head of a College, but commander of a beleaguered citadel. On May 29, a day of omen for the Stuart House, Lord Essex appeared, moving from Sandford towards Islip, and the King himself with Prince Rupert climbed the Great Tower to watch the development of his march. The danger passed by this time, to use the classic metaphor, "like a cloud," sweeping over Shotover and on to Otmoor, but sparing the city. But it came again the next summer, and yet again in the summer of 1646, when Fairfax delivered his final assault on Oxford. Did Addison, when some fifty years later he strolled up and down "Dover Pier," reflect that it had been so recently a scene of struggle and warfare ? Did any of the old Fellows tell him, as they well might have done, how it came by its name? College memories are singularly capricious in what they retain and in what they forget. This was the final agony, and if it was to come it was best it should not be longer delayed, for we can well believe that, as Wood says, the young men of the University had been demoralised by the life, "debauch'd by bearing arms and doing the duties belonging to soldiers, as watching, warding, and sitting in tipling houses whole nights together."

CHAPTER III

MAGDALEN UNDER THE COMMONWEALTH, THE RESTORATION, WILLIAM AND MARY, QUEEN ANNE, AND THE HOUSE OF HANOVER

THE " lost cause " was now finally lost. Oxford capitulated to the Parliament. There followed a period of disorder, filled with a noise of wrangling preachers, inquisitorial commissions, demands regular and irregular. To one of these last the mitre and staff of the founder, faithfully preserved through so many troubles, and valued at £2000, were surrendered and disappeared. The President, Dr. Oliver, was removed, and the Junior Proctor, a Magdalen man, withdrew under sentence. A new President was appointed, and a regular visitation of the colleges being held, Magdalen was the first to be visited, with the result that more than two-thirds of the Fellows and Demies, all the Chaplains, and a corresponding number of other members, foundationers and non-foundationers, were extruded and new persons introduced into their places. These were mostly Presbyterians. New hosts, new guests. Not many months after the King's death, Fairfax and the terrible Cromwell himself were to

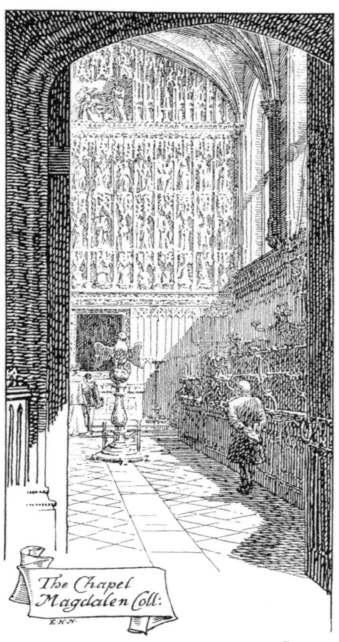

The Chapel
Magdalen Coll:

E.H.N.

D

be seen sitting at the High Table, on which the light streamed through the oriel window, where to-day, if not then, are to be seen the portraits of the ill-fated monarch and his Consort, presented in their happier earlier days, only sixteen years before. Whatever havoc was made, whatever destruction took place of painted glass, there or in the Chapel, these have escaped. They enjoyed, the chronicler tells us, very English fare, " good cheer and bad speeches." After dinner they and the Vice-Chancellor played bowls on the College green. It is possible that the Chapel windows, of which now only a few forlorn fragments remain in the Chapel porch, were destroyed a year or two later than this. But Evelyn did not notice the destruction when he saw the Chapel in 1654. What struck him was that the Chapel was "in Pontifical Order"—"the Altar only, I think," he says, "turned table-wise"—and that the double organ, "which abomination as now esteemed was almost universally abolished," was still in its place. This organ, it may be noted, was later on given to Cromwell, who had it at Hampton Court, where Milton may have heard and even played it. Cromwell seems to have offered them one in exchange from the banqueting-room at Whitehall. Coming back to the College with the Restoration [1] in 1660, it remained till 1737,

---

[1] " Pro transportando organo de Hampton Court, 16 li. 10s." Entry in Accounts of year 1660.

MAGDALEN COLLEGE

when it gave place to a newer instrument
and went to the Abbey Church at Tewkes-
bury, where it may still be seen, a slim,
symmetrical, graceful-looking piece. On
the whole, if some things were destroyed,
a good deal was allowed to remain. One
transaction, which as several who took part
in it discovered for themselves was of ques-
tionable propriety, was the division of Wainfleet's reserve fund of gold coins, laid up,
like the Periclean treasure at Athens, in
the Muniment Tower. Not a few of the
foundationers sooner or later voluntarily re-
funded their portion.

To the Presbyterians succeeded the In-
dependents. Parliament, when it appointed
one of this body to be President of Magdalen,
at least paid the College the compliment of
choosing a learned, a conscientious, and a
distinguished man in Thomas Goodwin.
He was from Cambridge, a Christ's College man, afterwards elected Fellow of St.
Catharine's, and he had been Chaplain to the
Council of State. But he was an oddity.
An avowed enemy of all earthly crowns,
and doubtless especially of the triple tiara,
he appears himself to have worn something
which looked like thrice three of the
famous *bonnets de coton* of the *Roi d'Yvetot*.
His portrait is still preserved showing him
in this quaint gear. The undergraduates
dubbed him " Nine Caps," and told good
stories about his unworldliness and oddity.
One of them was still current thirty years

52

later when Addison was a member of the College, and he has enshrined it in the *Spectator*, embalmed with the antiseptic spice of his own inimitable style.

"A gentleman," he writes, "who was lately a great ornament to the learned world, has diverted me more than once with an account of the reception which he met with from a very famous Independent minister, who was Head of a College in those times. This gentleman was then a young adventurer in the republic of letters, and just fitted out for the University with a good cargo of Latin and Greek. His friends were resolved that he should try his fortune at an election which was drawing near in the College, of which the Independent minister whom I have before mentioned was governor. The youth, according to custom, waited on him in order to be examined. He was received at the door by a servant, who was one of that gloomy generation that were then in fashion. He conducted him, with great silence and seriousness, to a long gallery which was darkened at noon-day, and had only a single candle burning in it. After a short stay in this melancholy apartment, he was led into a chamber hung with black, where he entertained himself for some time by the glimmering of a taper, till at length the Head of the College came out to him from an inner room with half-a-dozen night-caps upon his head, and religious horror in his countenance. The young man trembled, but his fears increased when, instead of being asked what progress he had made in learning, he was examined how he abounded in grace. His Latin and Greek stood him in little stead; he was to give an account only of the state of his soul ; whether he was of the number of the elect ; what was the occasion of his conversion ; upon what day of the month and hour of the day it happened ; how it was carried on, and when completed. The whole examination was summed up with one short question, namely, *Whether he was prepared for death ?* The boy, who had been bred up by honest parents, was frighted out of his wits at the solemnity of the proceeding, and by the last dreadful interrogatory ; so that, upon making his escape out of the house of mourning, he could never be brought a second time to the examination, as not being able to go through the terrors of it."

The story is doubtless based on truth, but bears pretty obvious marks of having been improved on, and shows that even the Independent undergraduates in the grim reign of the Saints were not wanting in spirits and humour. Stories not dissimilar have been told of ultra-evangelical Heads in much later days.

However, if eccentric, Goodwin seems to have been a good President, and the system of tuition and supervision prescribed by the Visitors was well conceived and produced creditable results. But neither had very long trial. In May 1660, as all know, the King "had his own again," and President Oliver and the ejected Fellows had their own with him, after just a dozen years of exile. A good silver-gilt cup, with a contemporary date and inscription, com-

memorates their "Restoration." But Dr.
Oliver did not drink out of it long. He
died in October 1661. His successor, recommended, it may be noticed, by the
King, was Dr. Thomas Pierce. His chief
memento in the College is a small silver
virge, still carried before the President. But
it could not be called a sceptre of peace, for
his term was mostly spent in fighting and
expelling various of the Fellows, with the
result of appeals and counter-appeals to
King and Visitor. As to one of these,
some of the Fellows pleaded their cause
in person before Charles II., who asked,
"Is your President really so bad?" "*Faith*,
your Majesty," replied Dr. Pudsey, their
spokesman, "he's intolerable." This made
the King laugh, and say, "He must be bad
indeed, since he makes this respectable old
gentleman *swear*." At last he agreed to
resign if made Dean of Salisbury, but only
on condition that Dr. Henry Clerke was
appointed his successor.

Clerke was not wanted by the College.
In particular, he had an old enemy in Dr.
Henry Yerbury, one of the chief thorns in
the side of President Pierce. But the King
desired his election, and elected he was. He
had, says Dr. Mew, one great advantage,
that "If he manages himself but tolerably
well, he will deceive the expectations of the
whole University." This he may be said
to have done. He seems to have been considered what would now be called "slack"

and *pococurante*. His portrait shows a singularly youthful, blooming, florid complacency, not unsuitable to such a disposition. But he was a person of some distinction, a Fellow of the Royal Society. He had been a careful Bursar, and he attended to the business of the College, and did not interfere too much —indeed perhaps winked rather hard at some serious abuses of manners and morals. He married his only daughter[1] well to Sir Richard Shuttleworth of Gawthorpe. It may be noted that he was the first Doctor of Medicine who had been made President, and he understood perhaps what all doctors of that day did not, the virtue of letting Nature take her course.

His reign was marked by several minor additions to the material amenities of the College. The old Chapel of St. John was turned into rooms, the vestry of the Chapel proper was converted into the Fellows' Common Room, the east end of the Chapel was decorated with painting and painted hangings by Isaac Fuller, and the organ repaired, while the Grove and Walks were taken in hand and gradually replanted.

When he died, the College, which he remembered in his will, admitted on his memorial tablet that he had brought back the peace which had long been wanting to them. It did not remain long undisturbed, though through no fault of theirs.

[1] She went in College by the name of the Infanta, and they were married in the College Chapel.

THE SECOND JAMES

"What is that college we are coming to?" asked, so the story goes, the Duke of Wellington, then Chancellor of the University, of Mr. Croker as they were entering Oxford together and Magdalen came in view. "That is Magdalen, against which King James II. broke his head." The expression was blunt but apt. Never was there a better example of the adage "*Quem deus vult perdere prius dementat*" than the infatuated folly of King James II.

That the history of one quiet college among some thirty colleges, as there then were at Oxford and Cambridge, should for the moment become part of the history of the country—this was a paradox which it required the peculiar combination of perverse and petty impolicy of the most perverse and least politic of the Stuarts to bring about.

He accomplished the task with extraordinary rapidity.

It was a paradox, too, in other ways. Neither the temper nor the tradition of the College was such as to bring it naturally into collision with the reigning House. King James had already procured by his mandate the admission of a Fellow, a convert to Romanism, Robert Charnock, who sided with him all through the subsequent contest. If the system of the royal "letter missive" had not become customary with the colleges as it had with the Cathedral Chapters, it was not far off becoming so. At Magdalen, in particular, Cardinal Wolsey, Edward VI., Queen Elizabeth, James I., the Parliament, and Charles II. had all interfered in the election or appointment of Presidents and had carried their men.

If King James's object was to secure a moderate Papist, with a little manœuvring he could probably have achieved this, as Queen Elizabeth did the election of the "Bond of Iniquity." But he gave the Fellows no chance. He did not even add insult to injury, but offered them both together as his first tender.

The story of the whole transaction has, of course, been amply written. Macaulay in particular has told it, if not absolutely accurately, with brilliant pictorial effect. By accident, indirectly, and for a brief time important to the nation, the struggle was certainly of immense importance to the College. It is no exaggeration to say that it was at one time a matter of life and death, for the President and Fellows were threatened with the dissolution of their beloved Foundation and Society. There is, however, no need to do more than give an outline of the transaction.

President Clerke died in Lancashire on March 24, 1687. The news in those days travelled slowly. It reached London first, through a private message sent by Lady Shuttleworth to one of the Senior Fellows, Dr. Younger, no doubt a friend of her father, and through him and Bishop Parker reached the King, who let it be known at once "that he expected the person he recommended to be favourable to his religion." The Vice-President and Fellows meanwhile had fixed the day for election, April 13, when a rumour reached them that the King

THE COLLEGE ARMS

had decided to recommend one Anthony Farmer. Farmer was in no sense a suitable person. He did not possess the statutable qualifications; he possessed every personal disqualification. He was a Cambridge man who had migrated to Oxford as a graduate, and somehow been allowed to creep into

Magdalen College by way of Magdalen Hall. He had little character, and what he had was mostly bad. If not thoroughly immoral, he was disorderly and dissipated. One of his least escapades had been to get into scandalous disgrace at Abingdon and throw the town stocks into "Mad Hall's Pool." What King James could hope to achieve through so poor and discreditable a tool it is difficult to understand. Fortunately the College had a candidate of its own, of ability, integrity, and resolution, Mr. John Hough, whose comportment during the troubles that immediately followed and whose whole subsequent career abundantly justified their choice.

After petitioning the King in vain to give them at least an alternative, they elected Hough and sent him off, galloping through the night, to Farnham Castle. The Visitor, who told him " he admired their courage," admitted him without delay, and on the second day after his election Hough was back again at College with the Bishop's confirmation in his pocket, was again sworn and installed, and took possession of the Lodgings. The College then again informed the King that Farmer was not eligible, that they were bound by the statutes to elect by the 15th, and that there being no other Royal candidate before them, they had elected Hough. They were cited to appear before the Ecclesiastical Commission, of which Judge Jeffreys was the President. The Commission declared Hough's election null, but even Jeffreys did not attempt to whitewash Farmer, but told him plainly "that the Court looked on him as a very bad man." King James, obliged to drop this candidate, directed the College to admit Samuel Parker, Bishop of Oxford, a respectable person, but, again, not statutably qualified. But now the Fellows replied that they "humbly conceived that the place was full." This brought the King himself in person to Oxford, where, at Christ Church, he rated the Fellows sharply and told them "to go at once to their Chapel and elect the Bishop of Oxford forthwith, or they should know what it is to feel the weight of a King's hand." They went to their Chapel, but in that solemn place they decided that it did not lie in their power to do what the King required, though they were "loyally ready to obey him in any matter not violating their conscience." At this point the well-known Quaker, William Penn, tried his hand as an intermediary, being strangely willing to aid the King in the promotion of Romanism. He failed, for Hough put the position in a nutshell when he said, "I see it is resolved that the Papists must have our College, and I think all we have to do is to let the world see that they take it from us, and that we do not give it up."

The King now determined to lay siege to the College with a regular battering-train,

and sent down certain Commissioners to sit
as Visitors on the spot. They met first in
the Hall and then in the recently constituted
Fellows' Common Room. The struggle
was dramatic. Hough and his Fellows,
strong in their rightful position, showed
both resolution and ingenuity in refusing
to be manœuvred out of it. The first act
ended with Hough's famous protest, delivered shortly after his name had been
struck from the books, in which he appealed
to the King in his Courts of Justice. The
scene is reproduced in Roubiliac's bas-relief
on the Bishop's tomb at Worcester Cathedral. It is true that this was not to be
carved until more than half a century later,
but it is not without historic value. It
shows the Common Room very much as
it still is, with the panelled walls and fireplace.

Hough withdrew to London, where the
old Countess of Ossory cosseted him up
as only a kind old lady can.

On 25th October the Commissioners
forcibly broke open the Lodgings and gave
possession to Parker's representative, and
they obtained from the majority of the
Fellows a sullen and negative acquiescence
that they would submit to Parker "so far
as was lawful and agreeable to the statutes
of the College."

But the King was what his Scotch
ancestors would have called *fey*. He required the Fellows to grovel and fawn.

JUS SUUM CUIQUE

He sent them a test formula to which they were to subscribe. Upon their refusal they were expelled to the number of twenty-five. Two new Fellows, both Romanists, nominated by the King, had already been admitted, some further admissions were made, and two young kinsmen of Bishop Cartwright of Chester, the chief Commissioner, were admitted Demies. The unfortunate Parker now essayed to rule the little province committed to him. The Demies declined to recognise either him or his Fellows, and " ran " the College routine for themselves. Still King James persisted. He added further Fellows, all Romanists ; he nominated new officers. When the Demies declined to recognise these, they too were expelled. Solitude and peace might now seem achieved, but one further melancholy circumstance was still wanting to complete the dismal chronicle. Parker, who perhaps never more than half liked his task, can hardly have been happy in his position. When early in 1688 he received a mandate from the King to admit yet another batch of Romanist Fellows, even his gorge rose. He fell into "a convulsive fit" and died. The King now had what he desired. He nominated Bonaventure Giffard, Bishop of Madaura *in partibus infidelium*, as President, and gave him authority to nominate and admit to all places in the College. The Roman service was introduced into the

Chapel.[1] Even those of the old Fellows who had hitherto acquiesced seem to have now revolted, and seven more were expelled. Giffard's portrait shows him as a lady-like old gentleman. He was not unlearned or unamiable, and specially charitable. But in any case he had no opportunity of making much mark. Oddly enough, like Hough, he lived to be over ninety, dying in 1733-34.

The triumph of the King and the new régime were short-lived. Circumstances had changed. The Dutch fleet was setting sail. He was persuaded to reverse his decision, and on October 11 directed the Bishop of Winchester, as Visitor of St. Mary Magdalen College, " to settle that Society regularly and statutably." Bishop Mew came to Oxford, and on October 24 struck off from the books the name of Bonaventure Giffard and all persons admitted during the last twelve months, and restored those who had been expelled.

Poetic justice has seldom been more complete. A few months later King James was himself a wandering exile. Neither he nor his direct heirs ever came back to the throne. The miserable end of Jeffreys is well known.

---

[1] The candlesticks now on the altar, by an odd accident, date from this time. The Chapel was robbed about a hundred years later, and the candlesticks stolen. In their place the College made use of the present pair left by Bonaventure Giffard.

Charnock, the one Fellow who had voted as King James wished from first to last, joined in a plot for the assassination of King William, and was executed.

Hough, the victim and the hero, became a marked man, known, as Macaulay says, in every parsonage in England, and designated for the preferment which his talents and character amply deserved, but for which under ordinary circumstances he might have waited long. He was made, almost at once, Bishop of Oxford, and enjoyed peaceably for nearly a dozen years the combination of dignities which had killed Parker in six months, was thence translated to Lichfield, and thence finally to Worcester, where he died far on in the next century, eulogised by Pope, esteemed and beloved by all who knew him. He had been offered Canterbury, but "*noluit Archiepiscopari.*" For,

" Why should Hough desire translation
Loved and esteemed by all the nation ? "—Pope.

Fairfax became Dean of Norwich. Holyoake, one of the ejected Chaplains, was afterwards a very successful Headmaster of Rugby School—one, indeed, of its three greatest Headmasters, says its historian.

It was part of the irony of the situation that the Fellows who so stubbornly resisted the King in regard to the one matter of the election were probably quite sincere in their protestation of general loyalty.

They were what Tom Hearne, Jacobite and Nonjuring, called "honest men"—that is, like Cicero's "good citizens," they agreed with the author of the epithet. More than one of those who had gone out and returned again lost their places rather than swear allegiance to William and Mary. Even as late as Gibbon's day, we know that the toasts of their successors were not "conspicuous for constitutional loyalty to the House of Hanover." Meanwhile their first task was to replenish the College and get to work again. In this they had no difficulty. After the storm follows the calm ; after the expulsion of the Demies came the so-called "Golden Election."

The disturbance of the years 1687, 1688 left a number of vacancies to be filled. No less than seventeen new Demies were admitted. Among them were Hugh Boulter, afterwards Dean of Christ Church and Archbishop of Armagh; Richard Smallbrook, afterwards Bishop of St. Davids and of Lichfield ; Henry Sacheverell ; and his chamber-fellow and friend, Joseph Addison.

The two Presidents who immediately succeeded Hough—John Rogers and Thomas Bayley—made no mark. After them followed President Harwar, whose portrait Hearne has etched in a few lines bitten in with his own acid, as "a Hypochondriacal Easy Person and good for little or nothing, who seldom appeared abroad, or did any

University duty, being a quiet man," but adds "that he is reported to have been very charitable." The College was still a Jacobite stronghold. When good Queen Anne died, some of its members again gave up their places rather than accept King George. The sentiment of those who remained is vouched for by a little episode which seems just made for a Jacobite romance, and reads indeed as though it came straight from one of Scott's novels.

When the King sent his famous troop of horse under General Pepper to teach the learned body of Oxford loyalty, one of his first steps was to invest the Greyhound Inn, a well-known hostelry, still remembered by living persons, standing just under the walls of Magdalen, on the site of the present School-Room. Here a certain Jacobite agent, by name Colonel Owen, whom Pepper was anxious to impound, was lodging. But some friend gave the alarm ; Owen had just time to jump out of his bed, and scrambling over the wall into the College, remained there for some days, hidden, tradition says, in the beautiful little bell-turret of the Grammar Hall, until his friends were able to get him safely away.

A college, however, is seldom unanimous, especially in politics. The next President, Dr. Edward Butler, was and did everything that Hearne disliked. He was "a very great Whig "; he was a layman, and remained so ; he married ; he turned the little Gothic windows of the President's Lodgings into "sash windows"; he was given to music and society, and allowed a "concert of music" to be held in the College Hall, and a "vast number of ladies" to be present. Notwithstanding all these enormities, he must be admitted to have been an able man and distinguished in the great world. He was Vice-Chancellor from 1728 to 1732, and he held a position which no other President of Magdalen, and few Heads of Houses, have held, that of University Burgess, from 1737 to the memorable year 1745, when he died. Possibly his taste for music may have had something to do with the replacing of the old organ, already mentioned, by a new one, the work of Thomas Schwarbrook.

It was in his reign, too, that the sepia-coloured windows from the Ante-Chapel were carried into the Chapel, and it was just at the end of his reign that one addition of great value was made to the treasures of the College, that of the nobly pathetic painting of our Lord bearing His Cross, which forms the altar-piece of the Chapel. Though it has been ascribed to Guido and Caracci, it is almost certainly Spanish, and Sir Joshua Reynolds told Dr. Routh he believed it to be by Ribalta. It was the gift of one of the greatest private benefactors of the College, Mr. William Freman.

The taste of the time—the eighteenth century had now, it should be remembered, definitely set in—was indicated by the sash windows in the President's Lodgings. The Walks and the Grove had gradually been replanted in the last quarter of the preceding century, and the idea of making the Grove a sort of gentleman's park had perhaps now entered into the College mind, for it seems likely that the deer were introduced

NEW BUILDINGS FROM THE GROVE

about the years 1705–10. Much greater changes and introductions were at hand. When Gibbon arrived on the scene, exactly in the middle of the century, his apartments consisted, he says, " of three elegant and well-furnished rooms in the new building, a stately pile ; and the adjacent walks, had they been frequented by Plato's disciples,

69

might have been compared to the Attic shade on the banks of the Ilissus." He admired them, he became fond of them, as he admired and liked the other amenities of the College, which he found ill exchanged for the Spartan entertainment of Protestant Geneva. "My spacious apartments in the new buildings of Magdalen College were exchanged for a dark, ill-furnished room in the most dreary street of an unhandsome city, and our domestic œconomy was dirty and penurious ; from the liberty and afflu- ence of a Gentleman Commoner I was reduced by my father's displeasure to the humiliating dependence of a schoolboy." And in their style the New Buildings are admirable, and not least so on their north side toward the Grove, less often seen than the southern view, far better certainly than any attempt at Gothic which could then have been made. The design was the work of an amateur, a member of the College, Edward Holdsworth, who had been Demy in 1714. He had achieved the fame which it was then possible to achieve with Latin poetry by a Latin poem. It was the age of Gray and Walpole. Like them, he had made the Grand Tour, and had im- bibed a taste, as so many did, for the Palla- dian models.

He was prepared to rebuild the whole College in this style, or at least to pull down the greater part of the Cloisters and erect a vast quadrangle to which the Chapel,

Hall, and Great Tower were to be joined.
Fortunately this was never done, and the
north side alone of the quadrangle, the
existing range of buildings, was erected.

Such was the College when Gibbon
came to it. Butler had passed away. The
President who had succeeded him, Jenner,
seems to have been a *roi fainéant*, and his
colleagues and subjects mostly followed his
example; for it must be admitted that all
the attempts made by Hurdis and others to
refute the charges of apathy and unpro-
ductivity brought by Gibbon in his famous
Autobiography have only served to demon-
strate their essential truth.

Gibbon, however, would have liked, as
he wrote himself in 1755, to get back to an
English University. And much allowance
must no doubt be made for the scorn of
extreme youth and the incompatibility of
genius. Gray and Walpole, a little later,
wrote much the same of Cambridge,
and West answered them from Christ
Church in a like spirit. Later still, Bentham
at Queen's and Southey at Balliol held
much the same language, while, nearer
our own date, Tennyson and Darwin at
Trinity and Christ's, and Clough at Balliol,
expressed themselves very critically of the
studies of the place.

There were, Gibbon admits, two, and
two only, of the members of the College in
his time whom he could except from his
charge of indolent ignorance; one was "a

half-starved Chaplain," as he calls him, in reality an academical clerk, George Ballard by name, who came to ask the well-to-do Gentleman Commoner to subscribe to a work he was bringing out on the *Learned Ladies of Great Britain*. A stay-maker with a taste for Anglo-Saxon, Ballard had, as his biographer says, "become, after quitting the external ornaments of the sex, a contemplator of their internal qualifications." The other was more important, "the only student," Gibbon styles him, "in College, a young Fellow" (a future Bishop) "deeply immersed in the follies of the Hutchinsonian system." It is at least creditable to Gibbon's college that it elected its only student to be President. This was George Horne, a devout, amiable, and sensible man, as his Life by another Hutchinsonian, "Jones of Nayland," amply shows. But we have less biassed evidence.

Dr. Johnson was acquainted with him. "We drank tea," says Boswell, describing Johnson's visit to Oxford in 1776, "with Dr. Horne, late President of Magdalen College and Bishop of Norwich, of whose abilities the public has had eminent proof, and the esteem annexed to whose character was increased by knowing him personally." Horne succeeded Jenner in 1768. Under his rule scholarship began to revive. Chandler published his *Elegiaca Græca* and his *Marmora Oxoniensia*, and went out under the auspices of the "Dilettanti Society" to pursue archæological research in Asia Minor, with results of high value for scholars. Shaw edited Apollonius Rhodius, with a value represented perhaps by the legend about " *Putide Shavius.*" Routh, to more purpose and with better fame, began to edit Plato.

Like almost every President, good or bad, Horne made alterations in the Lodgings. In particular, he removed the famous Election Chamber, the scene of Dr. Goodwin's lucubrations.

Another change, even more deplorable, has been after a hundred years to some extent repaired. The example of New College in 1790 seems to have led the College to doubt the stability of the roof of the Chapel and Hall, and to call in James Wyatt, who condemned it as insecure, and was commissioned by the College to replace it with a new roof of higher pitch, covered with slate instead of lead, and furnished inside with plaster ceilings imitative of stone groining. By the munificence of one of the Senior Fellows, Mr. H. F. Garnsey, the College, with Mr. G. F. Bodley, R.A., as their architect, has been able recently to cover the Hall once more with an open-work wooden roof, leaded and of the old low pitch. A fine window at the east end was at the same time reopened, restored, and reglazed, through the liberality of Mr. T. Case, Wainfleet Professor of Moral and Metaphysical Philosophy, and since President of Corpus; and the fireplace was rebuilt as a gift from the Estates Bursar, Mr. G. E. Baker.

Horne, a Kentish man, was for the last ten years of his presidency Dean of Canterbury. In 1790 he was made Bishop of Norwich. When he resigned, the College seems to have been determined on one thing, namely, to elect a junior Fellow and a young man. The contest lay between two such candidates, Martin Joseph Routh and John Parkinson. It is sometimes said that Routh, who had been delicate in his youth, was put in as a " warming-pan." They little thought that they were electing one who would become the oldest President the College had ever known.

What has chiefly impressed the public mind about Dr. Routh is his longevity. " The Head of my College," said " Bob " Lowe, " was a scholar and a gentleman, but he began his reign in the reign of Louis XVI." " I have just been up to Oxford to visit my College," said on one occasion Bishop Phillpotts, himself far on in years. " It is more than sixty years since I first went up to Oxford, and the same man who was Head of my College when I first went up is Head of my College now." And indeed the stretch covered by his life, or even his Oxford life, is such as to impress the imagination. Born ten years after Culloden, he was killed, it is said, by the fall of Russian stocks consequent on the Crimean

DR. ROUTH

War. He had shaken hands with a lady who had seen Charles II. promenading in Oxford with his spaniels. As an undergraduate he had watched Dr. Johnson's bulky form scramble up the steps of University. As a Fellow of Magdalen, he might have seen him enter the College on his visits to President Horne.

His whole life seemed laid out on a proportionate scale. He took a living and Priest's Orders when he was fifty-five ; he married ten years later, a lady whom he had baptized. He said "Sir" and "Sirrah"; he was one of the last in Oxford to wear a wig. In ever so many ways he retained the manners and habits of the eighteenth century far on into the nineteenth.

Pressed at the age of ninety-five to sit for his portrait, he said, "Wait till I'm a hundred, sir ; then I shall be a curiosity." He was in a sense a curiosity, but he was much more. His claim to consideration did not rest merely on his living like a tree. He was a real scholar and an excellent theologian, and continued to study all through his long life, nearly seventy years separating his last publication from his first. When the tradition of English Churchmanship and Theology was rediscovered, it was found that he was in advance of his age, partly because he had been before it.

Newman's well-known dedication to him, " reserved to report to a forgetful genera-

75

tion what was the Theology of their fore-
fathers," was no mere literary compliment.
His library, still preserved at Durham, was
that of a wide and deep student. His sug-
gestion to the Bishops of the American
Church to go to Scotland for apostolical succession, and not to Sweden, "where," he said,
" you won't find it, sir," was of some moment
in the history of the Church.

His counsel to Dean Burgon, " You will
find it a very good practice, sir, always to
verify your references," is one of the best
pieces of advice ever given by an older to a
younger scholar, and its value is not con-
fined to the region of scholarship. His
advice to Conington, if of less universal ap-
plication, is interesting : " Attach yourself
to some great man, sir ; many have risen to
eminence in that way."

It was natural that he should be a Tory
and highly conservative, and so he was,
though he had friends among the Whigs,
such as Dr. Parr and Sir Francis Burdett.

A great deal of his long reign was taken up
with building operations. Magdalen Hall,
the site of which the College had always
hoped to recover, was removed to the site and
buildings of Hertford College, the accidental
burning down of a large part of the Magdalen Hall premises in 1820 aiding the
transfer. The north side of the Cloisters,
which at some period or another had been
carried up to a third storey, was pulled down
and rebuilt in 1824, and in the next two

years two other sides of the Cloisters were rebuilt. The ends of the New Building were finished off in their present form. In 1828 the old Grammar School building was removed. Next the College called in Cottingham to restore the interior of the Chapel, the work being carried out during the years 1829–34. In 1844 Pugin's Gateway, men-

NEW BUILDINGS FROM THE SOUTH-EAST

tioned earlier, took the place of that of Inigo Jones. Finally President Routh's last public appearance was in connection with the rebuilding of the School by J. C. Buckler in 1849–51. About the same time the pious generosity of Mr. Roundell Palmer, afterwards Lord Selborne, who for a number of years gave up the income of his fellowship for this end, restored to the College Chapel what for centuries it had lost, coloured windows. The result of all these changes was to bring the College in the main into its present state, excepting for the addition of St. Swithun's Quadrangle, the rebuilding of the Lodgings, and the recent restoration of the Hall roof.

President Routh's theory was that the right of initiation of all measures, and perhaps the right of final veto too, rested with himself. He certainly did not initiate much, and if he did not exercise a formal veto, was a potent force in maintaining the existing state of things. While colleges like Oriel and Balliol and Trinity were reforming themselves and forging ahead, Magdalen remained in many ways stationary, and as the competition of such colleges gradually developed, perhaps even positively receded. Yet the old system attracted a good deal of talent, and many men of eminent ability passed through Magdalen during Dr. Routh's reign, more perhaps than at most periods of the College history. There was, too, a party of reform in the College, but they were not able to persuade the President. By-and-by, just in the middle of the century, their hands were strengthened by the action of Parliament and the well-known Commission. It was natural that to this Commission Dr. Routh should return a dignified *non possumus*. It was fortunate for his feelings that he was now at the end of his tenure of office. Just before Christmas

Day 1854, in the hundredth year of his age, in the sixty-fourth of his presidency, he was taken away from what he undoubtedly considered the evil to come.

He was succeeded by a Tutor and Fellow in the prime of life, a scholar and a musician, amiable, sensible, methodical, courteous, and of singularly fine and benign appearance, Dr. Frederic Bulley. Everybody welcomed him, for he possessed in a special measure one chief ornament of a College ruler. He was pacific. He lived through, and accepted, gracefully if not gratefully, the many changes in College and University which the new legislation brought about.

One of its first effects was to increase the number of the undergraduates. Instead of some dozen undergraduate Demies, there are now always something like the full thirty in residence; in the place of the few privileged Gentleman Commoners, the Commoners of to-day, whose numbers have gradually increased until they now exceed a hundred. The effect of this on the life of the College is obvious. It is remarkable how much had been done, how many interests kept alive, by the handful of undergraduates who lived in the College in the first half of the last century. The famous Union Debating Society was largely founded by two Magdalen men, Bishop Durnford and Lord Winmarleigh, as they afterwards became. The University Cricket Club in its early and humble beginnings was much aided by the then Master of the College School, and by some members of the College. But the College was too small to follow up either of these interests, and they passed into other hands. In the same way, though individual members of the College won laurels on the river, a College Eight was an impossibility. "In my day" (1840), writes an old Fellow, "there were in residence five undergraduate demies, four clerks, and four Gentleman Commoners."

To accommodate the increasing number, a new Quadrangle was begun in 1883, from designs by Messrs. Bodley and Garner, to which was given the name of St. Swithun's, after one of the Saints mentioned by the Founder in his foundation of the College.

Magdalen is even now, reckoning by the number of the undergraduates, not one of the largest of Oxford colleges. At least half-a-dozen are larger. But it is one of the largest Oxford foundations, and it is singularly varied in its composition.

Among the Fellows there are at present no less than seven different categories. Wainfleet's Prælectors are now represented by six Professors of the University who hold fellowships in the College. Instead of the old graduate Demies, there is the class of Senior Demies. The Chaplains are retained at their full number. There are nine Clerks, Academical and Lay. There is an Organist who is also *Informator Choristarum*, a Grammar Master and Usher, and a Steward.

Thus the original foundation, though modified more than once and in many points, remains in a sense intact ; and what is still more striking, the College in its general life and activity, in its contribution to the life of the University, and its place in the country, making allowance for changes of time and habits, will be found more nearly than at any intervening period to approach to what was its original state when it left the hands of its Founder, under the stormily gorgeous sunset of the Middle Age, and grew to its first strength in the dazzling dawn of the new day, amid the golden hopes and many-coloured enthusiasms of the English Renaissance and the English Reformation.

CHAPTER IV

COLLEGE LIFE DOWN THE CENTURIES

"A land of waters green and clear,
  Of willows and of poplars tall,
And, in the spring-time of the year,
  The white may breaking over all;
And Pleasure quick to come at call,
  And summer rides by marsh and wold,
And Autumn with her crimson pall
  About the towers of Magdalen rolled;
And strange enchantments from the past,
  And memories of the friends of old,
And strong Tradition, binding fast
  The 'flying terms' with bands of gold."
    ANDREW LANG, *Almæ Matres*.

A DISTINGUISHED Oxford man, still living, is fond of relating how, more than half a century ago, he one day went into Magdalen College Hall and saw there the venerable, old-world figure of President Routh, in wig, gown, and bands, standing under the picture of Bishop Horne. "You question, sir," said the old man, whose College memories went back more than eighty years, "what I am doing. I am regarding, sir, the portrait of my predecessor, and wondering with what sentiments my successor will regard mine."

So it is in a College, more palpably perhaps than anywhere else. Harry to Harry succeeds; the fleeting generations

82

come and go ; the home is the same, but the family is ever changing ; here more

THE FOUNDER'S TOWER FROM THE WEST

than anywhere else we realise how " Life," as the Roman poet sings,

" In lease is given to all, to none in fee."

And Dr. Routh's reflections naturally rise in our minds. What were our ancestors really like ? How did they live in this same College, in the early days more particu-

larly, and then down the different centuries?
Was their life at all parallel to that of the
present students, graduate or undergraduate?

Our evidence is scanty. We know their
life largely from two sources, their delinquencies and their debts, much as we know
some of the lost classics from the passages in
which the authors broke some grammarian's
rule.

In the very early days it must be remembered that the undergraduates were very
young and often very poor; poor schoolboys, we should call them. They stole apples
from the College garden; they stole sheep
from the Grove. They had the English-
man's love of sport, even in the form of
poaching. They kept not only dogs but
ferrets and weasels, sparrow-hawks and song-
birds, mavises and the like. Like Shakespeare
and his friends, they went deer-stealing, at
Shotover or Woodstock, and quarrelled with
my Lord's keeper. Those injunctions in
the statutes, at which the modern undergraduate laughs, about not carrying cross-
bows or playing childish or obsolete games,
were not made without reason.

They played at cards and "knuckle-
bones" for money. Peter Yate, B.A., sold
his "livery," or allowance for clothes, for
five-and-fivepence, which he proceeded to
lose at cards. Philip Kyftyll, Demy, played
at cards for money with the College butler.
They broke the windows by playing ball,
perhaps some rudimentary kind of fives, such

as that which the Eton boys played against the Chapel buttresses. They practised archery in the Grove. They threw the bar. Athletics in the modern sense are, of course, quite recent. Boat-racing was the earliest ; it came in a little later than the examination system in the last century. But boating in an unprofessional, simple way is, of course, much older. People used to sail to Medley as they now do to God-stow. This is mentioned in Wither's poems :—

> " In summer time to Medley
> My love and I would go ;
> For creame there would we call,
> For cakes and pruines too."

Antony Wood notes his visits there in 1657, and a year or two later ; and in 1691 Mistress Alicia Danvers, in her *Humours of the University of Oxford*, describes sailing to it :—

> " A place at which they never fail
> Of custard, cyder, cakes, and ale,
> Cream tarts and cheese-cakes, good neats' tongues,
> And pretty girls to wait upon's."

Wither, we may remember, mentions playing tennis. The game of " racketts " was also practised.

On March 12, 1683–84, Mr. Clerke, Commoner, " complain'd of Sir Chernock, Demy, for abusing him at Woods his rackett court, calling him *foole*, *Welsh Ambassador* (an expression for an owle), and otherwise vilifying him both *facto et verbo*." He was tried at two o'clock by the officers in "Præsident Clerke's dining roome," was judged "greatly guilty of the breach of the statute *Quod non sint conspiratores*," and was "putt out of Commons and allocation for a weeke." Alas! in the great world his assaults and conspiracies and penalties were to be far heavier.

"Bowls" is a very academic game, and the College "Bowling Green" is constantly mentioned in the accounts and records. It occupied apparently a level portion of the Grove, behind the New Buildings, which has since been used for lawn-tennis. On May 19, 1649, Cromwell and Fairfax, after dining with the new President in Hall, played at bowls with the Vice-Chancellor on the College green, and the same day, being doubtless in a gracious humour, ordered that Mr. James Baron, one of the new Puritan Fellows, should be created B.D. when he pleased. The "ingenious Mr. Addison," in one of his early Latin poems entitled "Sphæristerium," describes the place, the implements, the gesticulations, the plaudits, the perspirations and the imprecations, of his brother Fellows.

To return to general practices and earlier days, they shirked speaking Latin in Hall; they climbed the College wall; they cut lectures and chapels, and "vexed the souls of Deans." They were punished like schoolboys with floggings and impositions, and also, like undergraduates of a short time back before "Rollers" were invented, by being made to keep chapels, sometimes all the chapels there were—no light penalty.

Paul Browne, otherwise Sir Browne, as a Demy, " enveied against Calvin and Beza " ; he also blew out the candle at the disputations, and used odious words to the Dean of Arts. Yet good Queen Bess got him elected Fellow. William Barker, Demy, played " unseemly games," and sold his books to raise the wind. He was sentenced to sit in Hall for a week with uncovered head, fasting while the rest dined.

Mr. Ivory " had almost slaine the keeper's man which would not suffer him to hunte in the forest. He did jussell Mr. Wade and plucke him by the bearde in the Cloisters. He did also strike Mr. Merser, the Usher, in the Cloisters."

The Dons, too, had their foibles. The Dean himself sometimes cut chapel, and when taxed with it, said he was walking about College to see what undergraduates were absenting themselves. They practised the black art. A Vice-President was said by his enemies to have baptized a cat in order to discover hidden treasure.

There were the same differences between High and Low Churchmen. "Brother" Garret and "Brother" Edon of Magdalen used to attend Bible readings in Magdalen Hall, and distributed Lutheran tracts. For this Garret was arrested by the Vice-Chancellor at the orders of Wolsey, escaped from the Vice-Chancellor's rooms and fled towards Wales, was again caught and imprisoned, recanted, and was made to walk in procession, carrying faggots, and to burn his own tracts at Carfax. Then, with the turn of affairs, he came into favour and was made Chaplain to Bishop Latimer; then, poor fellow, when they turned yet again, was burnt at Smithfield.

They had their collective as well as their general amusements. Some of these were annual, such as the institution of the "Lords of Misrule" at Christmas-time, or the "Boy-Bishop" for the Choristers. They acted plays in Hall of very various kinds. In President Humfrey's time it seems to have been thought very edifying to act pieces showing up the folly of superstition.

Hospitality has always been one of the first duties of Oxford and her colleges. Magdalen began to exercise it even before she had a roof over her head, for a breakfast was given to Bishop Toly when he came to lay the foundation-stone of the Chapel. The College guests in early times were of every degree, and ladies were not excluded. President Mayew entertained his mother and sister, and the College cheesemonger, in Hall. A little later, in 1497, on a Sunday, when many guests were entertained, there were dining with the President the Abbess of Godstow, a nun, and another lady. Hermits, strange to say, seem to have been frequent guests. On one occasion a hermit and a plumber are entertained together. Royal visits were not rare. When Prince Arthur came to stay at the Lodgings, a good fire was made in the State rooms and a stock of torches laid in, money was expended on a store of red wine, of claret, and of sweet wine, and the little boy was given two pike and two tench. (If he lived like this at home it is not so wonderful that he never had good health and died early.) He was presented, like a modern judge, with gloves, a customary compliment to very distinguished guests. He seems also to have been shown some marmosets [1] to amuse him.

When the College lawyer visited the College he had better cheer than the Prince. He came at a better season, and was given herons, partridges, and quails for supper.

Sickness was common in College, especially of an epidemic kind. At times great fires would be lighted to keep off infection. The students had not separate rooms. They lived, as quite old Wykehamists can still remember living, in "chambers"; the Fellows occupying principal beds, the Demies and Choristers "truckle" beds in the same room. Sitting-rooms were of course unknown, and they packed much closer than inmates of colleges do now. Their private possessions were not great, as can be seen from their wills. A gown, a hood, a few books, a

[1] The spelling of this word seems to have taxed the College officers. They appear as "merumsyttes."

great box in which to keep them—such, like those of Chaucer's "clerke of Oxenford," were their properties.

Gradually, but only very gradually, did life become more luxurious. Even in the eighteenth century the representations of the rooms, as, for instance, in the *Oxford Sausage*, show them as singularly bare. A table, a chair, a box made up the bulk of their furniture.

In the early days there was little or no vacation. The institution of the Long Vacation came in about the end of the seventeenth century. But migrations for change of air were frequent. The bulk of the College would go for months at a time to Witney or Brackley. Bishop Fox arranged that the Corpus students should migrate to the same place as those of Magdalen, in order to attend the Magdalen lectures. Leave of absence could be granted for special reasons, but otherwise they resided the whole year round.

The Gentleman Commoners who paid for themselves had, of course, much more freedom. As every one remembers, Gibbon complained that he had too much, and could "elope" to Bath or London whenever he liked. They could also spend much more. The accounts of a young man of fashion, Mr. William Roberts, son of Sir William Roberts of Willsden, who came to Magdalen in 1655, show that he had, beside the ordinary furniture, a pair of globes, a tawny gowne, price £6, and a hat with a silver band, £2. He spent £478, 8s. 7d. in two years, including travelling and tradesmen's bills. But all this is nothing to the expenses of his wedding a few years after, when he became a Baronet and an M.P., when a present for his " Valentyne " cost him £12, a silver warming-pan £24, and a rope of pearls £252.

A great deal of money was expended on the trumpeters and drummers of Royal or noble visitors. On one occasion 10s. 6d. is given to a little boy who played a tambourine or banjo in the Hall, *puerulo qui in aula timpanizaverit*.

When Queen Elizabeth visited the College it was stuck over with verses and " emblematical expressions of poetry." The shrewd Queen prohibited plays, because they introduced the plague.

Among the goods of Henry Atkins, Fellow, in 1556, are described : " A gowne faced a littell before with taffeta, with a hoode belonging to the same, 20s. A habbett and a hoode lined with changeable sylk, a frock faced with conye, one other frocke faced with budge before, a hat of taffeta."

Bishop Morley's visitors in 1674, according to the gossiping Prideaux, inquired *inter alia* whether any of the scholars " weare pantaloons or periwigues, or keep dogs, but, which is most materiall in their inquiry, wither any buy or sell places."

The *menu* of the Hall dinner on mid-Lent Sunday is preserved. It is appetising. "A barrell of oysters, a dish of fresh fish, *videlicet*, a large jack, carp, tench, and perch, with oysters and anchovy sauce, 4 large chicken boyl'd with bacon and knuckle of veale, breast of mutton, a tansy, bak'd wardens, symnell and cheese." At the Gaudy dinner in 1589, three of the Master Fellows grabbed three of the best dishes away from the Vice-President. They were summoned before the President, who ordered them to supply others as good. A few years later the Bachelor Demies had to be punished for wearing hats instead of College caps at dinner in Hall.

The "Grove," "Virgultum," or "Arbustum," as it is commonly called in the College accounts or registers, has always been a characteristic feature of the College. In Agas' map of 1578 it appears as partly laid out in "Gardaines, Orcherdes, Pastures, and Walkes." The President and College officers seem to have had separate pieces as gardens walled off for their special use. Later it is not seldom alluded to, the most famous mention being Pope's happy adaptation of Horace's well-known line,

" To seek the truth in Maudlin's learned grove,"

which Gibbon perhaps had in mind when he penned his grandiloquently contemptuous comparison to Plato's disciples and the banks of the Ilissus.

West, the youthful friend of Gray and Walpole, the Oxford member of the "Quadrilateral," was much attached to both the Grove and the Walks of Magdalen. He

THE WATER-WALK

sent to Walpole, in April 1736, an Ode to St. Mary Magdalene, beginning—

> " Saint of this learned awful grove,
> While slow along thy walks I rove,
> The pleasing scene which all that see
> Admire, is lost to me " ;

and he writes to Ashton at Cambridge, " Have you any such walks as Maudlin ? "

Baskerville, a country squire who wrote a description of Oxford during President

93

Clerke's time at Magdalen, notes both garden and walks. He says, "This Coll : was brought to such perfection that nothing has been added to it in my time, and in some respects it doth exceed all other Colleges, for most of ye fellowes have convenient Gardens and private Stables, each man apart, for his own horse." He mentions also that they have a "Bowling Green," and "delicate walks of their own, of a great lenth, by Charwell, and when they please to stirr a little in those of ye Phisick Garden and up the Hill towards Hedington." Gibbon and his first and more amiable tutor used, it may be remembered, to take this latter walk on summer evenings.

The Magdalen "Walkes" also shared at this time with Merton "Walkes" the glory of being the resort of the "toasts," as they were called, and their beaux. Hearne, in July 1723, says that every Sunday in summer they were filled with these promenaders "just like a fair."

The trees in the Grove were probably planted in the time of President Clerke. There would seem to have been a maze in the Grove containing walnut-trees, which were cut out in 1702. About this date the deer apparently were introduced. There is an entry in the accounts of 1706 of £4, 2s. for killing the does in the Grove, and the same again in 1707. The College is found at different times keeping swans, but not, it may be assumed, black ones, as it does to-day; and in 1508 the King made a present to the College of a she-bear! In earlier days sheep were kept in the Grove.

Thirty years ago the Cherwell was still "bordured with crevisses," as Wood says. Now the crayfish have disappeared. The kingfisher fortunately, however, still haunts the Walks, and may be frequently seen, especially as the poet sings, in March, "flitting by under the barren bush"; and both Grove and Walks are frequented by many wild birds, wood-pigeons, woodpeckers, tits, wrens, nightingales, nuthatches, and so on.

Relics of bygone days may be seen in the old guns and pistols hung up in the old Bursary or Chequer. They went on progress with the Bursars, being used, not to extort the rents, but to guard them when obtained. In earlier days still, bows and arrows were used for this purpose, and the accounts of 1485 record the providing of a new case for the President's stock of these missiles.

Magdalen has perhaps always been a "show College." We find Antony Wood on June 3, 1657, paying 6d. to the porter for seeing the Chapel.

"The spacious gardens along the river side," writes Macaulay in his well-known description, "were remarkable for the size of the trees, among which towered conspicuous one of the vegetable wonders of the island, a gigantic oak older by a century, men said, than the oldest College in the

University." "The Founder's Oak," as it was sometimes called, is figured in Loggan's view of the College standing near the entrance to the Walks. A Somersetshire gentleman, Mr. Richard Paget, who was a Demy at the time, in a Diary still preserved at Cranmore Hall thus describes its end :—

" *Monday, June* 29, 1791. *St. Peter's Day.*— Between 3 and 4 in the morning the great oak fell down into the meadow, *nulli flebilior quam mihi.* The principal roots were entirely rotted off, so that 'twas a wonder it stood so long. Many hundreds of people came for several days to view it. The oak must have been at least 800 years old." The College decided to have a chair made out of some of the wood after a design by Mr. Paget, " for the use of Mr. President in the Hall." This chair, a very handsome one, is still preserved in the Lodgings.

The oak only exists in this secondary "avatar," but another "vegetable wonder" is yet to be seen, namely, the great Wych Elm in the Grove, said by experts to be one of the very largest trees of the kind in the country. It stands rather at the back of the Grove, and is consequently little known except to members of the College. When measured by Oliver Wendell Holmes, as he has so graphically recorded, in 1886, it showed a girth of 25 feet 6 inches at 5 feet from the ground.

OPEN AIR PULPIT

CHAPTER V

MAGDALEN COLLEGE CUSTOMS

MAY MORNING

Morn of the year, of day and May the prime !
  How fitly do we scale the steep dark stair,
  Into the brightness of the matin air,
To praise with chanted hymn and echoing chime,
Dear Lord of Light, Thy lowlihead sublime,
  That stooped erewhile our life's frail weed to wear !
  Sun, cloud, and hill, all things Thou fram'st so fair,
With us are glad and gay, greeting the time :

The College of the Lily leaves her sleep,
  The grey tower rocks and trembles into sound,
  Dawn-smitten Memnon of a happier hour ;
Through faint-hued fields the silver waters creep ;
  Day grows, birds pipe, and robed anew and crown'd,
  Green Spring trips forth to set the world aflower.

ON the 29th of May 1871—the day when, it may be remembered, the Magdalen College bells would be ringing for the Restoration of the Monarchy—Taine, the Protestant philosopher and historian of France, was in Oxford, a temporary exile, driven out by the domination of the Commune from his native land. He had just learned that Paris was that day in flames. He wrote to his wife : " I have been for an hour's walk in the High Street and in the streets behind Magdalen College. It is very beautiful, very calm, very classical.

99

It is like real theatre scenery. How fortunate these people are, and how unfortunate are we ! ''

The constitutional conservatism of Oxford and her colleges had struck in the same way a very different French observer some twenty years earlier. Dr. Bloxam was fond of relating how, when shortly after 1848 he took Henri Montalembert into Magdalen College Hall, the Comte exclaimed, looking at the portraits of Wolsey and Pole : "What, you have cardinals in your Hall. I thought this was a Protestant college ! " " Yes, we keep our cardinals, and are very proud of them," said Dr. Bloxam. " Ah ! " replied Montalembert, " in England you do not destroy the past ! " This has been the secret (may it remain so) of English progress. It has certainly been the secret of college history, in which nothing is so noteworthy as the intermixture of old and young, of the historic and the modern.

Many colleges possess customs of varying antiquity which have grown up during the years of their existence, some important, others trivial, some interesting survivals, or mementoes at any rate, of institutions or practices once significant, others accidental and almost meaningless. Magdalen has a good many, some genuinely venerable, others of very moderate or dubious antiquity.

One of the oldest and most interesting is the sermon in the open air preached from the stone pulpit on the Feast of St. John the

Baptist, June 24. This sermon is older than the College, and dates from the Hospital of St. John Baptist. When the College absorbed the Hospital it took over the duty of providing the sermon.

In wet weather, as Hearne's diary records, it was preached in the Chapel. About 1766 the practice of preaching it in the open air was given up. Various reasons have been alleged for this disuse, such as that a President caught cold and died—College tradition said that the "capital instance" was that of President Harwar, who died July 16, 1722, but the custom continued for many years after this date—or that the Quadrangle used to be decked with boughs in imitation of the wilderness, and that this led to an undue stripping of the walks.

It certainly was so decorated. "It is customary," says Hearne in 1716, "upon this day to preach in a Stone Pulpit in the quadrangle all beset with bowes, by way of allusion to St. John Baptist preaching in the wilderness"; and the accounts year by year show payments for such decoration.

But the real reason is doubtless that given by the famous "field-preacher," George Whitefield, in his letter to the Vice-Chancellor, of 1768. "I hereby appeal to the whole University, whether the Reverend Doctors of Divinity, Heads of Houses, Graduates or Undergraduates, ever looked upon it as criminal, or beneath the dignity of their place and station, to sit out in the open air on St. John Baptist's day to hear a Master of Arts preach from the Stone Pulpit in Maudlin College yard, though for fear it may be they should give further sanction to field-preaching they have lately thought proper to adjourn into the Chapel."

In 1896, after a silence of 130 years, a sermon was again heard in St. John's Quadrangle. Since then, whenever the weather has allowed, the practice has been kept up. A green velvet cloth, on which are embroidered the College Arms and mitre, with the date of the year (1617) when it first came into the College—" Le pulpit cloath " it is called in the accounts— is still hung before the pulpit or preacher's stall on the occasion of the sermon.

The other University Sermon in College, that given on St. Mark's Day, possesses less general interest. It was instituted as a commutation. Instead of a priest to celebrate Mass for the souls of Robert Perrot, formerly organist, Alice, Simon, and Elizabeth Perrot, it was arranged that one of the Fellows should be appointed to preach a " public sermon " in the College Chapel on this day, and that one of the Demies should deliver an oration in Hall on the Monday before the feast.

An amusing, if not edifying, scene took place on St. Mark's Day, 1688, when one of the Fellows introduced by King James II.,

Mr. Thomas Fairfax, was to preach. As Wood describes : " The bell rung and tol'd at Magd: Coll: for sermon at 10. At the same time St. Marie's bell rung and tol'd for the Vice-Chancellor, who had said beforehand, ' Wee shall then not be there to heare eulogies on the Virgin Mary.' At 10. Mr. Whyting of Wadham Coll: preached a good sermon, Fairfax's they say was but a dull one."

On the first Monday in Lent the President receives in Chapel 16d., the Fellows 8d., the Chaplains 6d., the Demies 4d., the Choristers 2d. apiece, from the benefaction of John Claymond, John Higdon, and Robert Morwent. This is now distributed, as far as possible, in " fourpenny bits," by the Bursar, during the singing of the Benedictus in a quaint metrical version, perhaps—so are ceremonies and uses intermixed in a college —a survival of the Puritanical régime.

Probably the most celebrated of all Magdalen customs is the singing on the top of the Great Tower at sunrise on the first of May. Many myths are still current about its origin and meaning—in particular, that it somehow represents a Mass sung for King Henry VII., who directed a payment to be made by the Rector of Slymbridge for the keeping of his "obit" on this day. With this legend Mr. Wilson has dealt very faithfully.

What is certain is, that the ceremony was set in order in its present form by Dr.

Bloxam about 1844. Somewhat before this the choristers went up in a very irregular manner, sang as they pleased, and often pelted persons below with eggs and other missiles.

The use of the hymn taken from the College Grace, written by Dr. Thomas Smith (Fellow, 1665–92) and set to music by Benjamin Rogers (organist, 1664–86), is said to have begun about the end of the eighteenth century. A little earlier than this the performance is described as "a merry Concert of both Vocal and Instrumental Music consisting of several merry Ketches and lasting about 2 hours."

Various mentions of some such performance carry back the tradition to the well-known allusion by Antony Wood.

"On the south side," he writes, "of the Chapel stands a beautiful and well-built Tower. . . . From the top of which, the choral Ministers of this House do, according to an ancient custom, salute Flora every year on the first of May at four in the morning, with vocal music of several parts. Which having been sometimes well performed, hath given great content to the neighbourhood, and auditors underneath."

How ancient was the custom? We cannot tell, but it seems not unlikely that it is as old as the Tower itself, perhaps as old as the College, perhaps even older. For it is evidently one among several similar customs which prevailed in Oxford and the neighbourhood. Antony Wood describes another which was followed by New College thus :—

"There was sometime an auntient custome belonging to New College fellows : viz., on Holy Thursday every year some of the fellows of New College (with some of their acquaintance with them) did go to St. Bartholmew's Hospitall and there in the chappell sing an anthem of 2 or 5 parts. After that, every one of them would offer up money in a bason being sett for that purpose in the middle of the chapell. After that, have some refreshment in the house. Then, going up to a well or spring in the grove which strew'd with flowers round about for them, they sung a song of 5 parts, lately one of Mr. Wilbye's, 'Hard by a cristall fountaine.' And after that come home by Cheney Lane and Hedington Hill, singing catches.

"The choristers and singing-men of New College," he continues, "did, in the morning about 2 or 3 (o')clock in the morning, sing an anthem on their tower ; and then, from thence to St. Bartholmew's."

In another place he gives a somewhat longer account, in which he says that formerly the day was not Ascension Day but May Day.

"The youth of the City would come here," he says of St. Bartholomew's, "every May Day with their lords (and) ladyes, garlands, fifs, flutes, and drumms, to acknowledge the coming in of the fruits of the year, or (as wee may say) to salute the great goddess Flora and to attribute her all prais with dancing and musick."

If this narration and explanation be accepted, it would seem to account not only for the singing on the tower, but for the blowing, still kept up, of the May horns by the populace, as being both parts of the original May Day celebration.

The disuse of the ceremony at St. Bartholomew's, Wood seems to ascribe to the destruction of the Grove at the time of the Civil War.

Dr. Bloxam, who regulated the May morning singing, also about the same time introduced, as a winter pendant, another custom, often supposed to be equally immemorial, the Christmas-tree with the singing of carols in Hall on Christmas Eve. This began as a private party in his own rooms, which became so popular that when he was Vice-President in 1847 he transferred it to the Hall.

An annual dinner on 25th October celebrates the Restoration of the President and Fellows on that day in 1688, while the loving cup and the toast, *Jus suum cuique*, also go round on 29th May to mark the more general and national Restoration of 1660.

Some other minor customs have disappeared ; a few have survived. Among those discontinued is the picturesque use by which the President on Maundy

Thursday washed the feet of seven choristers, giving them a penny apiece. The choristers further used to wait in Hall upon the Fellows and take part in the Grace. The waiting was kept up on the Gaudy Day within the recollection of many living. The singing of Grace still survives on that day, but on ordinary days not even the Chorister styled the "Aularius" now appears, and only his little stool in the corner of the Hall, by the High Table, records the vanished custom.

CHAPTER VI

MAGDALEN WORTHIES

ADDISON'S WALK

Green natural cloister of our Academe,
   What ghost is this that greets us as we pace
   Beneath your boughs, the genius of the place,
With soft accost that fits our musing dream?
Scholar, divine, or statesman, would beseem
   That reverend air, that pensive-brilliant face,
   And lofty wit, and speech of Attic grace,
Rich in grave ornament and noble theme:

'Tis he who played unspoiled a worldly part,
   Taught the town truth, and in a formal age,
   Lured fop and toast to heed a note sublime;
Who here had early learned the crowning art,
   To walk the world like Plato's monarch-sage,
   ' Spectator of all being and all time.'

THE grandest, undoubtedly, of all the sons of Magdalen is *Wolsey*,* " probably the greatest political genius," as Bishop Creighton says, " whom England ever produced "—England's Bismarck, who first made her a great Power, giving her in a few years a position she has never since lost; like Bismarck, too, in his sudden fall.

Shakespeare has indicated his salient features with a few master-strokes, and it must be remembered that Shakespeare was born only thirty-four years after Wolsey's

* Portrait in College.

death, and had doubtless talked with men who knew him well. He was a "scholar and a ripe and good one." And he was in

THE BELL TOWER FROM THE PRESIDENT'S GARDEN

a very real sense a Magdalen man, and owed more to his college than college worthies often do.

His picture in Hall is balanced by that of
*Cardinal Reginald Pole.** A better pendant
could not be, for a greater contrast could
hardly be found than that between the
rough son of the Ipswich butcher and the
courtly cousin of kings and queens. As
Tennyson makes Bishop Gardiner say :—

> " Pole has the Plantagenet face,
> But not the force made them our mightiest kings,
> Fine eyes—but melancholy, irresolute—
> A fine beard, Bonner, a very fine full beard,
> But a weak mouth, an indeterminate."

The " thrice noble child of the College's
own bosom," the College called him. His
great hour was when on St. Andrew's Day,
1554, he swept up the Thames in a royal
barge, with a silver cross sparkling at the
prow, to reconcile his country to Rome.
Seldom, says James Gairdner, has any life
been animated by a more single-minded
purpose.

The two most important of Magdalen's
alumni in literature are one whom she never
forgets, *Joseph Addison,** and one whom she
hardly ever remembers, *John Lyly*. With
all the difference between the age of Anne
and of Elizabeth, they have not a little in
common. " I have brought philosophy,"
wrote Addison, " out of closets and libraries,
schools and colleges, to dwell in clubs and
assemblies, at tea-tables and in coffee-houses."
" Euphues," said Lyly, " had rather lie shut
in a Ladye's casket than open in a Scholler's

studie." "He was averse," says Wood, "to
the crabbed studies of logic and philosophy,
and his genie being bent to the pleasant
paths of poetry, he did in a manner neglect
academical studies." Like Gibbon, he says
that he himself was neglected. "The
Maister and the Schollers, the Tutor and
the Pupill be both agreede," he writes, "for
the one careth not howe lyttle pains hee
taketh for his money, nor the other how
little learning." But he wrote in a palinode :
"I think there are few Universities which
have less faults than Oxford, many that
have more, none but have some."

What more do we know of John Lyly ?
He was a smoker (then a new thing), he
played the fiddle, and he did not pay his
batells very regularly. Truly the marks of
a "poetic genie."

Another Elizabethan member of Magdalen is "resolute *John Florio*," a friend of
Daniel, and probably also of Shakespeare,
who borrows from his Montaigne.

John Foxe (1516–1587) was for a while
Fellow and Lecturer in Logic at Magdalen.
Then, with several other Puritans, he left
the College "for an honourable reason of his
own accord," and went to Frankfort to make
a third to Knox and Cox. His great *Boke
of Martyrs* was meant to be, and was, a
popular work. He sent a copy of the book
to the Library, where it may still be seen.

He also sent his son Samuel, his "little
Fox," to the College. Little Samuel for

some reason took to fine clothes and, it was said, to Popery, and was expelled, but his father got him restored by Royal mandate.

It is one of the great glories of Magdalen (thanks to President Humfrey) to share with Merton *Sir Thomas Bodley*. He was a Lecturer in Greek and Natural Philosophy, a Proctor, and Deputy Public Orator. Then he went into the great world as a courtier and diplomatist, enjoying by turns the favour and flouts of Queen Bess. He heard one day, " for his comfort," that " she had wished in her wonted Tudor fashion that I were hanged." At last returned and retired, " I set up my Staffe," he says, " at the Library doore in Oxford, being thoroughly persuaded that in my solitude and surcease from the Commonwealth affairs, I could not busy myself to better purpose than by reducing that place which then in every part lay ruined and waste, for the publique use of students."

Sir Thomas Roe * deserves a word of notice : one of the very earliest makers of the Empire, who, as Ambassador to the Great Mogul in 1614, commenced the British penetration, not destined to remain always peaceful, of India. A little later he was Ambassador at Constantinople, and described the Turk as " the sick man." " Honest Tom," the Queen of Bohemia called him, but the cynical motto affixed to his portrait savours of the line and trade of Wotton and

Metternich and Bismarck. Perhaps he deceived by telling the truth. He was a friend of Ben Jonson, and a poet himself.

Dr. Peter Heylyn wrote the Royalist story of the War. Of "mean port and presence, a bluster-master, conceited and pragmatical," he had opinions, and the courage of them. Against persecution, poverty, and blindness, he bore bravely up. Critical and controversial, but independent and loyal, he is a useful authority. Of Magdalen, at any rate, he deserved well.

"Lovely *Wither*," a contemporary poet called him. "A prodigious pourer forth of Rhime," Winstanley wrote of him, "which he spued from his maw as Tom Coriat spued Greek." Both criticisms are true. He will always be remembered by one song, as good in its way as any in the language—

> " Shall I, wasting in despair,
> Die because a woman's fair?
> .   .   .   .   .
> If she be not fair for me,
> What care I how fair she be ? "

Of his Magdalen days he has left some record in his poems. He describes how he made acquaintance with

> " The palaces and temples that were due
> Unto the wise Minerva's hallowed crew,
> Their cloisters, walks, and groves : all which
>   surveyed
> And in my new admittance well apaid,
> I did as other idle freshmen do,
> Long to go see the bell of Osney too :

> And yet for certainty I cannot tell
> That e'er I drank of Aristotle's well,
> And that perhaps may be the reason why
> I know so little in Philosophy."

He goes on to say how he "atchiev'd some cunning at the tennis-ball," and how his tutor tried to draw him to a love of what he taught.

Then his father took him away from Magdalen—why we know not.

> " By false appointment that no stay can brook,
> The Paradise of England I forsook.
> The sweetest of my hopes I left, and went
> In quest of care, despair, and discontent,
> For seeing I was forced to leave those mountains,
> Fine groves, fair walks, and sweet delightful foun-
>   tains,
> And saw it might not unto me be granted
> To keep those places where the Muses haunted,
> I home returnèd somewhat discontent,
> And to our Bentworth's beechy shadows went."

Pious, prophetic, pragmatical, polemical, prosaic, prolix, he swamped himself in the flood of his own verbosity. "Don't kill Wither," said the jolly Cavalier Sir John Denham ; "while Wither lives, I shall not be the worst poet in England." But he was a true poet at times, and his prison-notes, as Lamb says, are finer than the wood-notes of his poetical brethren.

Of Magdalen Puritans the greatest and the best is *John Hampden.** His mother, a Cromwell, wanted to see him wear a coronet. In their youth the Puritan gentry were as ready for *L'Allegro* as for

Il Penseroso. "At his entrance into the world," says their famous historian, "he indulged to himself all the license in sports and exercise and company which was used by men of the most jolly conversation." Later he retired "to a more reserved and melancholic society, yet preserving his own material cheerfulness and vivacity, and above all a flowing courtesy to all men." That he was on the eve of sailing with his cousin Cromwell to America is not established ; but if he did not sail thither his ideas did, and the poet is justified in tracing American Independence to Hampden's example.

> " Whatever harmonies of law
>   The growing world assume,
> Thy work is thine, the single note
> From that deep chord which Hampden smote
>   Will vibrate to the doom."

When he drew the sword he "threw away the scabbard." His "green coats" had for their motto "God with us," but also *Vestigia nulla retrorsum.* The story of his death has been alluded to. Richard Baxter thought it added a new attraction to heaven.

If there were those who did not like Dr. Fell, but could give no reason, there were those whom Dr. Fell liked, and with excellent cause shown. Such was "the most learned, reverend, and pious *Dr. Henry Hammond,*" Fell's life of whom the *D.N.B.* describes as one of the most charming pieces of biography in the language. His true bent and the life of his choice are best described by one who followed them, the author of the *Christian Year*, who, coming a pilgrim to his graveside, wrote thus :—

" Meek, pastoral, quiet souls, whoe'er ye be,
Who love to ply in peace your daily task,
Nor of your gracious God find aught to ask
But what may help you to eternity.

  .   .   .   .   .   .

Come take your rest with these by holy Hammond's side."

Another Magdalen divine of those days, a notable benefactor of the College, was good *Bishop John Warner*.*

Among the Fellows ejected in 1687 several were men of some mark. Notable in the annals of the College is *Dr. Thomas Smith*, "Tograi" or "Rabbi" Smith, as he was called for his Oriental learning. A more jovial companion, if a less strenuous soul, was *Henry Fairfax*, who ended as Dean of Norwich. "Go to him when you will, you will find him walking about his room with a pipe in his mouth and a bottle of old strong beer (which in their country they called Nog) upon the table, and at every other turn he takes a glass." The sketch is by his successor in the Deanery, Humphrey Prideaux.

Addison * is the ideal Magdalen worthy. It may be said, indeed, that he is in his own line the ideal of the academic char-

acter. Wherever he went, he was still
the Oxford scholar.

> " For wheresoe'er I turn my ravished eyes,
> Gay gilded scenes and shining prospects rise,
> Poetic fields encompass me around,
> And still I seem to tread on classic ground."

"Classic ground": he invented the
phrase. Beyond it he never wished to
wander. If · he appreciated the romantic,
it was because, as he had the wit to see,
there is romanticism in the classics too.

Magdalen cherishes his memory as she
forgets that of Gibbon. Though Addison's
rooms have perished, she remembers their
position; [1] Gibbon's are still standing, but
she cannot point them out.

He "commenced poet" with Latin
poems on Magdalen subjects. The first
English poem he published is subscribed,
"Mag: Coll: Oxon., the Author's age 22."
Dryden, to whom it was addressed, en-
couraged the "most ingenious Mr. Addison
of Oxford." Another early piece is addressed to "Dearest Harry," his brother
Demy, Henry Sacheverell. The story of
his sudden apotheosis is told so that it
cannot be bettered, by another Carthusian
author, Thackeray, in that most charming

[1] On the north side of the Cloisters rebuilt in 1820.
They were pointed out by Dr. Theophilus Leigh to
President Routh. Dr. Leigh came up in 1708, when
Addison was still a Fellow. Dr. Routh died in 1854,
146 years later.

of historical novels, *Esmond.* It is worth noting, perhaps, that the famous hurricane,

"Such as of late o'er pale Britannia past,"

which puffed the *Campaign* into prosperity, wrought signal devastation at Magdalen—blew in the west window of the Chapel, detached two pinnacles from the Tower, and wrenched a large branch from the Founder's Oak.

He sleeps in the Abbey, among whose monuments his Spectator mused so memorably. Magdalen possesses several portraits of him, and several relics. And for such as love him his gentle ghost still seems to walk the shadowed avenue where he paced so often in life, meditating perhaps those lines into which he rendered the verse of his favourite psalm—

"Where peaceful rivers soft and slow
Amid the verdant landskip flow."

Among those who have had, if not greatness, at least notoriety, thrust upon them, none is more conspicuous than *Henry Sacheverell.** Son of a poor parson, godson of an apothecary at Marlborough, he was elected Demy along with Addison, and became his "chum." He was impertinent to the Dean of Arts, but in due time was elected Fellow and became Dean himself. His famous sermon on "Perils from false Brethren" was, *more predicantium,* only an old Oxford discourse touched up. Parliament impeached him, and made him a hero or a martyr. He was condemned, but the Whigs lost office. It must have been a notable day for his College when the " Doctor " rode over Magdalen

St Swithun's Buildings

bridge escorted by his admirers, five hundred strong, on his way to the living his friends had given him in Shropshire. His portrait in the College Hall shows a self-satisfied, personable man, sulky perhaps and mutinous, but hardly forcible enough for turbulence.

*Hugh Boulter,** successively Dean of Christ Church, Bishop of Bristol, and Archbishop of Armagh, was also one of the " Golden Election." His portrait, which hung long in the Hall, and hangs now in the College School, represents him, at least as large as life, relieving the Irish poor, both satirically described by Swift.

" Observe that lovely form ! see Boulter's hand
Stretched out to save from misery the land.
Behold that group ! now freed from all complaint,
They praise, they bless, they hang upon the saint."

A satellite of the Dii Majores, but himself a very minor shade, is the *Rev. Thomas Yalden,* preserved to an exiguous immortality in the stony Mausoleum of Johnson's *Lives.*

Yalden presented to the College a large, expensive, well-meant, very imaginary portrait of the Founder.* It displays him as he certainly never was, but is interesting as showing what the eighteenth century thought he might have been.

A poet of a very different order is *William Collins.* Gilbert White of Selborne gives us a few traits and stories. He found college life slow ; he went home gaily dressed, and with a feather in his hat, and called on his cousin Payne, and when cousin Payne hinted at extravagance he spoke of him as a d—d dull fellow. He gave a tea-party in his rooms. A " ragging " brother Wykehamist from New College kicked over the

table. Our poet, though of a warm temper,
took it very well, and getting up from his
chair, calmly began picking up the slices of
bread-and-butter and the fragments of his
china, repeating very mildly—

" Invenias etiam disjecti membra poetæ."

His " Ode on the Manners " seems to
describe his leaving Oxford for London.
Now was his brief heyday. He went to
the Guildford Races. He made love to
Miss Bett Goddard, and inscribed to her an
Ode on the death of Colonel Ross, killed
at Fontenoy. He made the acquaintance
of Johnson, of Thomson, Quin, Foote, and
Garrick. Johnson describes with wit and
affection his life of debts and duns. He
came into a small fortune, £2000, which
" Collins could scarcely think exhaustible,
and which he did not live to exhaust."
Thomson put him into the *Castle of Indo-
lence*. In return, when Thomson suddenly
died, Collins wrote the lovely Elegy which
immortalises them both.

" Remembrance oft shall haunt the shore
    Where Thames in summer wreaths is drest,
And oft suspend the dashing oar
    To bid his gentle spirit rest."

No poet has struck more truly the note
of the Thames valley and stream—that note,
as a later Oxford poet happily says, " gently
echoed by Wordsworth in commemoration
of Collins' own sweeter song and sadder
end."

That sad end came very quickly, in a melancholy, worse than Gray's "leuchocholy." His last view of Magdalen Tower was taken, it is to be feared, when, as a friend saw him, he was being "dragged from under Merton Wall in the arms of two or three men" to a madhouse in St. Clements. He died at Chichester two years later. Peace to his gentle, mournful memory.

> "Yet once again, dear parted shade,
> Meek Nature's child, again adieu!"

"Oxford," says Mr. Swinburne, referring to Shelley, "has turned out great men in a double sense." The story of Gibbon has been already touched on, and every one knows it as etched by himself for all time, with such biting acid and so firm a stroke.

Of note in science are *Gowing Knight*, a distinguished Fellow of the Royal Society, a researcher into electricity and magnetism, and an improver of the mariner's compass, appointed in 1756 the first Principal Librarian of the then new British Museum, and last but not least, the inventor of venetian blinds; and *Dr. Edmund Cartwright*, now forgotten as a poet—though Sir Walter Scott called his "Armine and Elvira" "a beautiful piece"—but remembered as the improver of the power-loom and the inventor of a wool-combing machine.

The beautiful plane-tree which stands between the Lodgings and the New Buildings records the bursarship of *Henry Philpotts*,*

afterwards the famed fighting Bishop of
Exeter, who planted it there in the first
year of the last century. Of those who
followed him as members of the College
during its earlier half, a fair proportion are
memorable. It must be remembered that
they were a very small band. Only one
other became an English Diocesan, *Richard
Durnford*, born in 1802. At Eton his school-
fellows wrote of him—

" What is genius ? Durnford, tell ! "

At College the most brilliant scholar of
his time, a great rider, swimmer, and
cricketer, and one of the founders of the
Union Debating Society, later an admirable
parish-priest and Prelate, he literally died
young at ninety-two.

A divine of a different sort was *James
Mozley*, Professor of Ecclesiastical History,
in worldly matters innocent almost to the
point of being ludicrous, but a rare mind
who made a deep mark on the theo-
logical temper of his time. Unworldly
also, learned and conscientious, was *William
Palmer*, who, disquieted by the qualms
and questions of that restless era, when
the Orthodox Church would not receive
him, found shelter in the bosom of Rome.
His brother, *Roundell*,* a still better scholar
and a Churchman no less conscientious,
who came in as a Fellow from Trinity,
became the most distinguished Magdalen
man of his day before the great world. His

portrait by Ouless hangs in the Hall. A genius fitfully more brilliant, but less steadfast, his razor-edged intellect almost too keen for foe and friend, and at times even for himself, was his brother Wykehamist, *Lord Sherbrooke*, better known as " Bob " Lowe.

A notable Gentleman Commoner was *John Wilson*, afterwards known as " Christopher North." There was nothing of the "crusty Christopher " about him when he was at Magdalen, unless indeed it were the port of his " Ambrosian evenings." He was like one of Ouida's heroes ; he leapt the Cherwell, doing, his biographer says, 23 feet ; he walked from a London dinner-table back to College through the summer night ; he played the French horn, he won the Newdigate, and wound up with a brilliant examination for his degree. Poet, philosopher, and critic, and Professor of Moral Philosophy at Edinburgh, he became the friend of Wordsworth and Coleridge and De Quincey. Of splendid physical and mental force, he was, as a poet himself too little known sings, "a man magnificent," though he achieved little.

> " A few pale poems and some worthier prose
> Make up the meagre sum which the world knows
> Of what was working in that mind and breast :
> The vague eternal kingdoms have the rest."
> *Elleray*, by J. TRUMAN.

A more fastidiously beautiful writer and a better philosopher was his son-in-law, also a Gentleman Commoner, *James Ferrier*,

author of the *Institutes of Metaphysics.*
Scholarship and letters have been well
served by two Demies who were at Magdalen together in the "forties," but both of
whom she unfortunately allowed to migrate
elsewhere — *John Conington,* Professor of
Latin, and *Goldwin Smith,* Regius Professor
of History.

A bizarre and Bohemian figure among
the Fellows of Magdalen was that of the
author of *Masks and Faces* and the
Cloister and the Hearth — *Charles Reade.*
A man of conspicuous physique, uncon-
ventional and theatrical, affecting as Vice-
President the green coat with brass buttons
of the old-fashioned English country gentleman, to whose class he belonged, he was a
scholar who, when he wanted to advocate
ambidexterity, could quote his Homer. He
was also a fiddler and a collector of fiddles.
Comparable to Defoe and Dumas, "the
greatest master of narrative since Scott," it
is thus that Mr. Swinburne writes of him,
and concludes : "At the best, and that not
very rarely, a truly great writer of a truly
noble genius." Magdalen will remember his
happy dedication of one of his best works
"To the President, Fellows, and Demies of
St. Mary Magdalen College, Oxford, by a
grateful son of that ancient, learned, and
most charitable house."

From her earliest days and the institution
of Wainfleet's Prælectors, Magdalen has
been a home of Natural Science, and in

particular of Botany. Since the modern development of these studies she has attached to herself many conspicuous names, such as those of *John Phillips* and *John Obadiah Westwood* and, latest lost and not least, or least loved, *Sir John Burdon-Sanderson*.* But her own children during the first half of the last century were *Lord Rosse*, the owner of the famous telescope and President of the Royal Society, and, still more representative, *Dr. Daubeny*,* a real pioneer of science in Oxford.

Time would fail to tell of other worthies. A word, however, must be said of a very conspicuous and characteristic line. The Magdalen Choir, said a partial friend from another college, has always been good. The sequence of its Organists is certainly remarkable. *Benjamin Rogers* * and *William* * and *Philip Hayes* * (1734–1777 and 1777–1797) are among its most shining links. Their zeal has been as remarkable as their genius. Only one of them perhaps, the redoubtable John Shepparde (rightly named), in 1553, ever went so far as to kidnap choristers and bring them home in chains; but the same spirit of devotion to the choir has animated them down the ages.

And if good in old days, the choir may claim to have become still better in the last century. Only three organists died during that period. The first two, *Vicary* and *Blyth*, were notable in their day. But to the third, *Sir John Stainer*,* belongs the credit of having given music the place and potency it enjoys in the English Church to-day. And in this work Magdalen preluded St. Paul's.

His successors, *Sir Walter Parratt* and *Dr. Roberts*, still fortunately live, and the chronicler must not anticipate, however well assured, the day, yet distant, it may be hoped, of their *éloges*.

But, after all, if a college is known by its great men, it should be judged rather by its rank and file. Magdalen should be estimated not by Wolsey or Hampden or Gibbon or Collins, nor even altogether, typical as he is, by Addison himself, but by the more domestic figures of those who have lived and died for her within her walls, and the more average characters of those who, taking her impress upon their temper, have worn it quietly in the more usual ways and walks of life. She owes more perhaps to none than to one of these forgotten worthies, a Fellow of the earlier Magdalen Hall, one of the three Bachelor Fellows of the College at its foundation, *Richard Bernes*. He died at the age of 100, having lived in the reigns of two Richards, two Edwards, and four Henrys, and been Vice-President for thirty years. Among his goods when he died were "a feather-bed, a good painted chest, twenty-four books, and many little boxes filled with evidences." He superintended the erection of the most important portion of the earliest and best buildings of the College, the Chapel, the Hall, and the Cloister Quadrangle.

WILLIAM COLLINS

Nightingale poet, all too delicate
  For the world's noon ; shy scholar, with the fair
  Vision of ancient Hellas and the rare
Magic of her lost lyres impassionate,
Thou for a while of freedom, love, and fate,
  Nature and man's regret, didst trill thine air,
  Thy bosom to the thorn, but couldst not bear
Of raptured frenzy the o'erteeming freight :

Yet for thy suffering guerdon large was given,
  In weakness to forerun corrival strength
  And catch the music of the coming days :
From thy mad cell to hear the voice of Heaven
  After earth's Babel, and on earth at length
  Pure laurels and thy brethren's nicest praise.

THE COLLEGE ARMS [1]

The College arms appear to be a combination of the coat of the family of Patten with the lilies of the Virgin Mary, these last perhaps adopted by the Founder when Headmaster or Provost of Eton.

The technical description is as follows : " Lozengy sable and ermine, on a chief of the first three lilies argent, stalked and seeded or."

As is often the case, there have been at all times slight variations in the blazoning. The diamond-shaped pattern on the shield sometimes appears as "lozengy," sometimes as "fusilly." The shape and colour of the lilies also vary, they being sometimes shown with green stems and foliage.

The most authoritative form, if not the most beautiful, is that given to the College in 1574 by Richard Lee, Portcullis, for which, as the College accounts still show, the College paid the herald forty-five shillings ; it gives the lilies " stalked and seeded or." Richard Lee also adds a motto used by Wainfleet and his College—*Fecit mihi magna qui potens est et sanctum nomen ejus.*

[1] See page 59.

INDEX

ADDISON, Joseph, 2, 46, 53, 66, 86, 110, 116–118, 127
Agas' map of 1578, 92
Altar candlesticks, the, 64 n.
Altar-piece in Chapel, 68
Altars and ornaments removed, 33
Alterations made in Chapel by Frewen, 40
Annual dinner, 106
Anwykyll, John, 14
Arms of the College, 129
Atkins, Henry, clothing of, 91

BAKER, G. E., 74
Ballard, George, 72
Barker, William, sentence on, 87
Baskerville's description of Oxford, 93, 94
Bernes, Richard, 127
Bible readings by Tyndale at Magdalen, 29
Bishop Fox, 26
Bloxam, Dr., anecdote by, 100 ; 104, 106
Bodley, Sir Thomas, 36, 112
Bolton, Henry, 32
Bond, Dr. Nicholas, 36, 39
"Bond of Iniquity," the, 36, 37, 58
Book of Common Prayer accepted by College, 33
Boswell's description of Horne, 72
Botanic Garden, 8
Boulter, Hugh, 66, 120
Boundary wall of College, building of, 13
"Bowling Green," 86, 94

Bowls played by Cromwell and Fairfax on the College green, 51, 86
Browne, Paul, 87
Bulley, Dr. Frederic, 79
Burdon-Sanderson, Sir John, 126
Butler, Dr. Edward, 67, 71
Byron, Sir John, 43

CALVIN, introduction of theology of, 33
Cardinal Beaufort, 11
Cartwright, Dr. Edmund, inventor of wool-combing machine, 122
Case, Professor T., 73
Chaloner, Sir Thomas, 38
Chandler, works published, 72
Chapel of College, 2, 4, 13, 14, 25, 30, 32, 40, 51, 64, 68, 77, 118
Charles II., 55, 58, 75
Charnock, Robert, 57, 65
Choir Practice Room, 5
Christmas revels at College, 88
"Christopher North" (John Wilson), 124
Churchmen, High and Low, 87
Claymond, Dr. John, 26, 27, 103
Clerke, Dr. Henry, 55, 58, 86, 94
Clock, contract for a College, 25
Cloisters, the, 14, 37, 38, 41, 70, 76, 117 n.
Colet, John, 26

131

INDEX

INDEX

133

INDEX

INDEX

St. John's Quadrangle, 4
St. Swithun's Buildings, 5
St. Swithun's Quadrangle, 4,
  78, 80
Scholars, two bodies of, 16;
  disorderly conduct of, 35;
  life in early days of, 84
Selborne, Lord. *See* Palmer,
  Roundell
Shakespeare, 14, 84, 108
Sickness at College, 89
Smallbrook, Richard, 66
Smith, Dr. Goldwin, 19, 125
Smith, Dr. Thomas, 104,
  107, 116
Stainer, Sir John, 126
Stanbridge, John, 14
State Bedrooms, 5
Statues in Cloisters, 41
Statutes, the, 17, 18
Swinburne quoted, 125

Taine at Oxford, 99
Tapestry presented to the
  Lodgings, 25
Tennyson quoted, 115
Thackeray, W. M., 117
Toly, Robert, Bishop of St.
  Davids, 14, 88
Tonsure abolished, 30
Tybard, William, the first
  President, 13, 17
Tyndale, William, 29

Union Debating Society,
  founding of, 79, 123
University Cricket Club, 79,
  80

Venetian blinds, inventor
  of, 122
Vestments for Chapel, 30
Violent demonstrations in
  Chapel, 30

Wainfleet, William, 6, 7,
  9–11, 13, 17, 20
Warner, Bishop John, 116
" Water-walks," the, 2, 41,
  42, 69, 93–95
Wellington, Duke of, 57
West, verse by, 93
Westwood, John Obadiah,
  126
White, Gilbert, of Selborne,
  120
Whitefield, George, letter
  of, 101, 102
William of Wykeham, 10
Wilson, John ("Christopher
  North"), 124
Winmarleigh, Lord, 79
Winstanley quoted, 113
Wither, George, 39, 42, 85,
  113, 114
Wolsey, Cardinal, 26–28,
  58, 88, 108–110, 127
Wood, Antony, 40, 95, 103–
  106, 111
Worthies of Magdalen, 108
  et seq.
Wych Elm in the Grove, the,
  96

Yalden, Rev. Thomas, 120
Yerbury, Dr. Henry, 55
Younger, Dr., 58

THE END

Printed by Ballantyne, Hanson & Co.
Edinburgh & London

For EU product safety concerns, contact us at Calle de José Abascal, 56–1°,
28003 Madrid, Spain or eugpsr@cambridge.org.

www.ingramcontent.com/pod-product-compliance
Ingram Content Group UK Ltd.
Pitfield, Milton Keynes, MK11 3LW, UK
UKHW012339130625
459647UK00009B/405